ROBERT M. GOLDWYN, M.D.

Beyond Appearance:

Reflections
of a Plastic Surgeon

DODD, MEAD & COMPANY

NEW YORK

To my parents,
my wife, and my children

Library of Congress Cataloging-in-Publication Data

Goldwyn, Robert M.
  Beyond appearance: reflections of a plastic surgeon.

  1. Goldwyn, Robert M. 2. Plastic surgeons—Massachusetts—Cambridge—Biography. 3. Physician and patient. 4. Harvard Medical School. I. Title. [DNLM: 1. Surgery, Plastic—personal narratives. WZ 100 G62495]
RD27.35.G65A37   1986   617'.092'4 [B]   85-25426
ISBN 0-396-08669-1

You live and die according to what goes on in yourself, which no one else can ever begin to know, not even father, mother, wife, son, or daughter.

—*William Saroyan*

Acknowledgments

I am grateful to Helen Rees, who encouraged me to write this book; to Nancy Love, who greatly improved it; to Cynthia Vartan at Dodd, Mead, who perceived its possibilities and helped me to realize them; and to Catherine Finn for her careful copyediting. Don Kalick thoughtfully read the near-final draft and made many corrections and suggestions.

My thanks go also to Anita LoConte for enduring the many drafts; to Jane Sivacek for assisting in this unglamorous process; and to Elaine Feuer for typing the ultimate version.

I appreciate receiving permission from the Harvard Medical Alumni Bulletin to quote from my talk, "Once Upon a Time ... There Was No Part-Time."

To preserve confidentiality, I have changed patients' names, occupations, and residences. In a few instances I have presented as one patient a composite of two. However, everything in this book did happen.

My views and observations are not necessarily those of any institution or organization to which I belong.

Introduction

This book is about the process of plastic surgery, about some of my patients and myself, and about our relationship. It is not an autobiography although it is autobiographical; it is not an ode to me or a manual for someone contemplating a facelift. My purpose is to tell what it is like to be a plastic surgeon caring for patients. I think of myself as "caring for" instead of "taking care of," which unpleasantly connotes a custodian or animal keeper. I have avoided also "dealing with patients," since it suggests working in the complaint department of a retail store. The phrase "treating patients" is not what I have in mind because that implies a one-way relationship of doctor to patient and nothing reciprocal, as if the doctor is a remote dispenser of salves or surgery.

In an ideal interaction between patient and physician, each benefits beyond the obvious: not only does the patient get well and the physician get paid but the patient enjoys the competence and kindness of someone committed to his well-being. And the physician receives satisfaction from exercising skills and from enlarging a personal universe through aiding another human in difficulty.

Despite the patient's illness and the doctor's knowledge, they are ultimately equal in their fragility; yet so strong is the power of denial that many doctors, especially if they are healthy, believe they are invincible, secure beyond disease, disintegration, and even death. For all of us the truth is otherwise, but unconsciously, we physicians are so fearful of our own vulnerability that we try to protect ourselves by ministering to others. This bargaining finally fails; cemeteries are clogged with negotiators.

The mutual realization by patient and physician that they are in life's flux together is an essential ingredient in doctoring. Although patients want their doctors to be strong shamans, they also appreciate a modicum of humility. The patient then feels less misunderstood and less grotesque.

Being cognizant of one's ultimate powerlessness is an uncommon mental stance for most doctors. We have been schooled to control and direct our emotions. Imperturbability and equanimity have been cultivated for centuries with bonzai devotion. It is not a far step from being as solid as a rock to being as cold as a stone.

Self-exposure, though necessary for this book, has been difficult for me, as it would be for most doctors, who consciously avoid baring themselves to strangers; we are accustomed to having others do that in front of us. My problem in writing this book was not so much in finding the correct words—although some might disagree—but in shedding my carapace. Plumbing the core-self is painful.

Many accounts of plastic surgery, including those written by plastic surgeons, ring false. The authors seem to have been preoccupied more with image than with truth.

In this book what I have recorded may be partly idiosyncratic. Nevertheless, I believe most plastic surgeons who read what I have written will acknowledge its veracity but will also regret my spreading on the lawn some items that are usually kept in the house.

To give a realistic idea of what it is to be a plastic surgeon, I have described in sequence and in detail the many events of a full working day. Although an observer may think that I am behaving in a way totally consistent with my professional role, many unprofessional things are happening beneath the surface: thoughts, motives, drives, and conflicts that I, like many other surgeons, often struggle to modulate in order to function effectively.

For me and, I suspect, for most of us, a day is not linear. Affected by the past, we live in the present, anticipating the future. We are not single-cell organisms. Our complexity enables us and forces us to act and react to a situation at various levels of our being simultaneously. While we may seem to be doing a particular task, we may be thinking of something remote. In this book, I have tried to divulge these different layers of activity and these various dimensions of self.

This book is also about Harvard Medical School and one of its hospitals, where I work. I talk about being on the fringes of the medical establishment, as a plastic surgeon who does both aesthetic and reconstructive surgery.

What we who work within the Harvard aegis think of our institution depends upon our individual experiences, our successes and frustrations, not only in relation to

ix

Harvard and a particular hospital but in relation to other aspects of our life, such as our health and family.

In this book, I do discuss some major problems that beset medicine in general and Harvard in particular: the enervating skirmishes between full-time, hospital-based doctors and part-time practitioners whose offices are outside the hospital and whose medical income is almost solely from private patients; the alarming rise in malpractice suits and the fear and cost engendered; the financial pressures on the Medical School, its hospitals, and all doctors to remain fiscally viable despite government cuts in payment for medical care; the personal need to be sufficiently flexible to adapt to rapid change and yet maintain superior standards.

Whatever the larger issues—in medicine, at Harvard, on this planet, or in outer space—I, as a plastic surgeon, still have to get up in the morning to do my work and to live with dreams and love. I also have to age while helping others look as if they are not. Except for the last, these realities are true for my patients as well. That is also what this book is about.

chapter 1

7:00 A.M. *Monday.* I cross the moat from home to hospital. I cannot change the earliness of the hour, but I can transform my mortgaged house into a medieval castle, my shared driveway into a lowered drawbridge, and my worn Olds into a fresh mount. Converting reality into something more desirable is what I, as a plastic surgeon, do professionally for others and personally for myself.

The census takers make the same mistake every decade when they count me as one. In fact I am a conglomerate: middle-aged male, physician, plastic surgeon, husband, father, son, relative, friend, neighbor, acquaintance, employer, citizen, a white, and a Jew. Each self I have had to accept with varying degrees of enthusiasm and reluctance. The sum of me is less than the aggregate of the parts, imperfectly welded into a structure cumbersome but unique, soon to converge on a patient, who is also a multiple and one of a kind.

If the police should question my neighbors, they would say, "He always leaves between 6:30 and 7:15 in the morning—every day except Sundays."

This regularity is a necessity but also an embarrassment. Nurtured by a romantic mother and weaned on Kipling and Hemingway, I seem to have gone astray, but not inexplicably. Early I identified with my father, a psychiatrist, hardworking even at eighty-three, and stable, not the befuddled type of the usual therapist jokes.

When I was in college, one of my professors characterized France as a combination of the Gallic and the Gothic spirits, the practical and the impractical, the sturdy and the soaring, the peasant and the poet. I did what going to college was supposed to do for me: I referred the metaphor to myself, recognizing that I also had these elements and that they could injure or enhance, depending upon what I did with them.

Now at this hour, with a workday beginning, the utilitarian in me takes over, as it must in order for me to drive to the hospital, especially in Boston traffic. A confession: I do not use my seat belts although I dutifully recommend them to my patients and my family. Why do I resist, after having witnessed so much facial trauma? An adolescent rebellion, a death wish, an only child's fatuous protest against doing the expected and being like others?

This part of the day belongs to the joggers. Most of them are young, but there is an occasional oldster trying to walk quickly, looking stiff and self-conscious like someone who has just separated from his wife and is going through the divorce rituals of dieting and exercising. The back of his shirt should say, "Now Available in a New Edition." I am cruel when I should be more understanding, since much of my work is changing the book jacket.

In ten minutes, I have reached the Beth Israel Hospital, where I park the car and enter the lobby of this major teaching center of Harvard Medical School, from which I graduated thirty years ago. I have been in the system so long I have made the cycle—medical student, resident, instructor, professor—and am back again to being an old student, learning from colleagues, nurses, *real* students, residents, and others who work at the hospital or in my office. While I have more prestige than ever, and more apparent power, I also have more vulnerability. Any mistake I make is more visible. I have to learn new techniques and, even harder, new attitudes. When working with those younger, I am conscious of the pressure of bending with the times while remaining affable and maintaining standards.

The functioning of a hospital emphasizes the crucial interconnections of the older with the younger, of physicians with nonphysicians. While those who are senior may direct those junior, a hospital hinges on the young. A strike of the under-thirty-five would cause a standstill.

My title is head of the Division of Plastic Surgery, a position I have held for twelve years. It sounds awesome, but it isn't. My service, though busy, is small: two other plastic surgeons, a chief resident in the final year of plastic surgical training, and an intern on a monthly rotation with us.

I spend a significant part of my life in this lazaretto, modern in its care, feudal in its functioning. Today more people leave a hospital than die in it, a significant difference from the hospices of the Middle Ages. Over the entrance of what remains of one of them in LaTour, France, are the words: *"Elas, Fauf Morir"*—"Alas, One Has to Die."

The hierarchy of the modern hospital is unambiguous. The differences between patients and others are clear, and there are administrators to make these distinctions still clearer. What is ambiguous about a hospital is what can happen to a patient. Correct diagnosis is not always easy, and treatment not always successful. A healthy adult, for example, may die during what should have been a routine hernia repair. This basic uncertainty that pervades all medicine becomes obvious in the hospital, where it causes tension but also engenders excitement. While we doctors may complain of the professional stresses, we secretly revel in the brinkmanship. In the emergency room, saving a patient in shock from a stab wound is an experience that a young surgeon never forgets. Mingled with the fear of failure, there is the awareness of being crucial. For a terrible moment, you feel more alive as the patient is becoming less alive. Finally, if the victim survives and pinks up as his circulation returns, you also have a suffusion, a peculiar pleasure that only a combination of fatigue and success after near-defeat can give.

In the lobby of my hospital, I greet a psychiatrist whom I occasionally meet here on his way to see his first patient. Now in his late fifties, he immigrated many years ago from South Africa, as so many Jewish physicians have done, feeling disenfranchised, fearing another catastrophe, another Nazi Germany. Athletically built, fond of swimming, he is vigorous and certain in his manner and work. His particular interest is hypnotherapy, and his pragmatic approach to the mentally ill might once have

4

distressed some of his older colleagues who were more Freudian.

"I could have been a psychiatrist, too," I muse, for the most part glad that I am not. But I am also slightly envious of their being able to sit long enough to contemplate life, while I must hurtle from place to place.

When I was young, I wanted to become a psychiatrist like my father. At Harvard College, I majored in clinical psychology and sociology, then called "social relations," a peculiar term that implied to my family that I was having more fun with people than I actually was. I wrote my honors thesis on aggression and used a picture test to measure hostility in delinquents at a reform school; the control group was a class at a boys' club. I was disappointed not to find any difference in aggression between the two groups. Either that observation was true, I concluded, or my test was poor, failing to reach a more meaningful stratum of the personality. I became more aware of the complex nature of the human being, who functions or dysfunctions at various levels, sometimes simultaneously. After college, I entered Harvard Medical School and set my direction toward psychiatry, until my third year, when I actually took my first psychiatric course. Our instructors taught us to submerge ourselves when we were with a patient, to remain inconspicuous, to elicit facts, emotions, and motivations without being obtrusive. Never could we openly direct a patient, and under no circumstances could we offer an interpretation.

Diffidence had not been a desideratum in my rearing. My parents and I valued a personal style that was open and colorful, by our admittedly middle-class standards. To me it seemed unnatural to let the patient spend months or even years trying to change his or her behavior by acquiring insight that I could give them in much less time. I found it arduous to limit myself to an occasional "yes" or "tell me about it" or repeating the question that the patient had just asked.

Nowadays, psychiatry has changed; therapists are not so inert or unresponsive. They are even armed with drugs, which my father had always advocated from his anti-Freudian stance. His indoctrination, he admitted, had come from his uncle, Dr. Boris Sidis, once a well-known psychiatrist and author who ran a private sanitarium in Portsmouth, New Hampshire. A friend of William James, he had not only a medical degree but also a doctorate in psychology from Harvard.

That my father was directive in his therapy and even used medications did not provide me with a strong enough example to become a psychiatrist. From all that I had been taught at Harvard, I concluded that, if I were to take a psychiatric residency there, I would have to dance to the psychoanalytic tune. My father, I reluctantly realized, was not au courant, although his patients liked and respected him and got well. He occasionally embarrassed me when I brought home college classmates who, like me, had been inundated by Freudian concepts. He would say, "You are being taught by psychologists who have never had to deal with ill patients and someday there will be a pharmacologic cure for mental illness, especially the manic-depressive disorders. They are now being treated inadequately or worse and by artificial, invalid precepts. Even Freud would have advanced and would not have accepted blindly what his followers have taken as gospel."

I would smile indulgently at my father and nervously at

my friends, who probably admired me for having overcome such an inhospitable, Philistine environment. Time, of course, seems to have vindicated my father and humbled me—a not so surprising sequence for parents and children. Fortunately, my father lived to see the medical progress that he had predicted.

As a medical student taking psychiatry, despite my growing alienation, I was aware of its major advantage. If I said something wrong to the patient, my instructor allayed my guilt by telling me that it was "grist for the mill. You can take it up next time." It was unlike surgery, where wrong cuts are irrevocable.

One incident from those days has remained with me. I was walking through the corridor at what was then the Boston Psychopathic Hospital, now the Massachusetts Medical Health Center, with one of my patients, a twenty-year-old student. He stopped in front of the Coke machine and offered to buy me one. His gesture startled me. How can I accept something from a patient in therapy, I wondered. Was he being kind or manipulative? Fortunately, I remembered that the amount of therapy I was doing for him was minimal and my instincts overcame my scruples. In addition, I had no change. He gave me my Coke, but when his came out, it had only syrup at the bottom, an error in the bottling. "See," he said, "if I told my therapist [the attending psychiatrist] what just happened, he would never believe me or would say that I am paranoid."

Now, about thirty years later, as my psychiatric colleague and I diverge in the lobby, I can truthfully say that I have no regrets over my career choice. I have maintained my identification with my father by choosing the most psychiatric of surgical fields; yet I have separated from him sufficiently to have the satisfaction of building my own career.

I was blessed with a father who always encouraged me, was never competitive, and, in fact, used to say that I had more ability than he had—a gross exaggeration. Nevertheless, I benefited from his modesty. Perhaps my experience with my father was unusual; it did not prepare me for subsequently witnessing the enormous ambivalence some fathers have toward their sons' successes.

As I wait for the elevator, I observe those around me. If one is a people-explorer, there is always entertainment. Noticing others, their physical and emotional characteristics, and trying to assess their personality and motivations have value in my work and, more important, give me pleasure. I can remember, as a child of ten, sitting with my parents in a restaurant and presenting my evaluation of those who passed by. My mother would want to know the type of person I thought he or she might be: likes and dislikes, whether hostile, flamboyant, generous, or happy. My father wanted more objective information from me: presumed age, height, weight, hand dominance, possible occupation, and gait abnormality or signs of disease. This preparation was helpful for medical school, although at the time I enjoyed it because of my Sherlock Holmes mania, a condition that still afflicts me.

The adverse influence of this hobby was to judge someone prematurely and perhaps unfairly and incorrectly. Yet most human encounters, certainly those between physician and patient, depend upon swift appraisal.

I enter the elevator and say a few words to a couple of doctors and a nurse. Anyone who can converse in an elevator—when most are mute, staring self-consciously upward, watching the floor numbers—must be an egotist. But it is a rare surgeon who is not. Most of us have a readily identifiable presence, not always pleasing, but assuredly there. We do not slither silently. A surgeon is the kind of person who goes to the bathroom within earshot of others and doesn't let the water run to muffle the sounds.

Plastic surgeons are less crescendo than general surgeons. We are somewhat different because we are supposed to be more artistic and aesthetic, more aware and appreciative of beauty in nature and in the human form. If a plastic surgeon lacks these inclinations, he will try to acquire them because of his desire to fit a stereotype that is pleasing to himself and comforting to his patients, who feel reassured when they learn that their plastic surgeon's hobby is sculpting, for example. Surely this kind of individual, they think, will give them the best result.

When I was in the process of deciding on a career in plastic surgery, I worried about my qualifications because I never had talent in drawing. That fear abated when I met older, successful plastic surgeons who had the same deficit.

I do have an aesthetic sense when it concerns my work, women, and art, but I block out physical surroundings, small items like the out-of-doors! I used to delude myself by thinking that my selective perception was a protective device: if I were constantly aware of my environment, I would see too much that was ugly and regret it. I reasoned that, although there was an Ashcan School of art, I, even as a plastic surgeon, could not inwardly transform a littered sidewalk into something beautiful.

I later realized that my aesthetic sense is a matter of compartmentalization, a specialty with me. Now I work; now I play; now I see this; now I don't. When it is a question of my profession, to which I have a fervent devotion, I can easily push my "aesthetic" button. It takes little for a male surgeon to appreciate female beauty. But to go beyond lust, to define physical beauty, and to struggle to bring it forth through operation, is a different matter, requiring study and training.

Plastic surgeons are probably less macho and obtrusive than our cardiac or orthopedic counterparts. Plastic surgery is not the cornerstone of medicine but the bas-relief.

The plastic surgeon is to surgery what the psychiatrist is to medicine: an outsider, not in the mainstream. As a matter of fact, when I told my chief of surgery at the Peter Bent Brigham Hospital, Dr. Francis D. Moore, that I was going into plastic surgery, he was surprised and referred to it as the "backwaters." He was right, but I felt the need to free myself from the turbulence I perceived was associated with general surgery. I believed also that, unless I could master the area in which I was working, I would not be happy. Dr. Moore had done this with general surgery, but I thought I could not imitate him because of his brilliance and the large scope of the field. I knew myself well enough to realize that I would be more comfortable and more productive by narrowing my focus, acceding to my inclination toward being intensive rather than extensive. I could manage my boat better in a rivulet than in a river.

Some older chiefs of surgery still have an animosity toward my field. One of them recently asked, "Why should I give a top spot in my general surgical program to someone who will later become a plastic surgeon and will just bob noses and play with tits?" The causes of their hostility are many: their view of plastic surgery as trivial because it seldom saves lives and includes cosmetic surgery, which they consider frivolous; their perception of the cosmetic patient as vain and entitled; their resentment and perhaps secret envy of the high fees that the surgery of appearance garners.

Before I decided upon plastic surgery, I realized I would be an outsider, but that position was not new for me. To be a Jew is to be an outsider. Going into plastic surgery would merely compound the problem or the advantage, depending upon one's viewpoint. That a Semitic background could be an obstacle soon became evident. Upon the advice of Dr. Joseph E. Murray, then the distinguished chief of plastic surgery at the Brigham (an energetic man of many accomplishments, including the first successful human renal transplant), I applied for plastic surgical residencies away from Boston, which had none. Two chiefs of service wanted to know my religion, and although I responded, I resolved not to join either of them because I felt that their query was degrading. It was also inconsequential information as far as I was concerned. Why should religious affiliation influence a decision about an applicant's potential to be a good plastic surgeon, or anything, except perhaps a deacon?

Eventually, I went to the University of Pittsburgh Medical Center, which had one of the best plastic surgical programs in the world. Its director, Dr. William L. White, thought in terms of an individual's achievement, not pedigree. In that respect, medicine has changed for the better. Evidence of this evolution is abundant in the elevator I am now taking. Those with me are a black obstetrician, a Chinese male resident, and two female doctors, one in surgical training and the other an internist on the staff.

I get out on the twelfth floor, where most of my patients are admitted. This morning a security officer is standing in front of the elevator, checking everyone's identification card. I am not wearing mine, for reasons that are irrational—in the seat-belt category. I prize individuality and resist classification, probably another peculiar legacy of being an only child. There is another explanation, one that I would worry about if I were a psychiatrist and heard it from a patient. I associate these identity cards with the armband of the Nazi era. Am I the only one in this Jewish hospital to make this connection? Fortunately, I need not compromise my idiosyncrasy since this particular guard recognizes me.

I have come to see in consultation a seventy-year-old man who has a recurrent basal cell carcinoma of his forehead. His doctor, who is a general surgeon, really should have referred the case to a plastic surgeon, but he is the kind who never lets a patient evade his surgical gloves unless he is on Medicaid. This surgeon wants to know how I would "handle it," to quote him.

Mr. Frank Cronin is a short, muscular man with sandy hair and old sod in his speech. He still works as a gardener for the same family that hired him when he came to this country a half-century ago. The sun exposure has furrowed and roughened the skin of his face. Mr. Cronin represents the kind of patient who is disappearing from the urban teaching hospital. He is respectful and trusting. Do these adjectives patronize him? Some might say that he is the type of patient whom medicine exploits, but I believe he would elicit the best from his doctors, who would appreciate his respect and strive to earn it. It is satisfying to be Mr. Cronin's doctor not because he will "not cause trouble" but because he appears devoid of distrust.

Mr. Cronin has the skin that could consume the efforts of a legion of dermatologists. Many years of sun exposure have produced atrophy and innumerable premalignant growths. The lesion of his forehead has already been biopsied and will require a moderate excision that can easily be done under local anesthesia. A flap of skin and fat from nearby will rotate into the defect resulting from removal of the cancer. Like many things in plastic surgery, the procedure is not difficult once conceived. Mr. Cronin's doctor need only incise on the lines that I have drawn. If I thought that he could not do the operation, I would tell the surgeon. This would involve an unpleasant interchange no matter how politic one might strive to be. Mr. Cronin does not seem apprehensive about his operation. He also understands my role in his care.

"I'll be sure, doctor, that he cuts where you want." He laughs collusively.

I go back into the elevator, down to the record room to settle accounts. I am almost as obsessive about these matters as are the staff in the record room, whose motto could be: "If it has not been recorded, it has never happened." Historically, the patient archives started as a convenience, became a nuisance, and now, in this litigious age, are a necessity. I sign my discharge summaries and operative notes almost without reading them, an unwise practice even though it saves me time. Working in the record room are many young people trying to get through college. There are also one or two widows who prefer to spend their nights here rather than at home alone. To most physicians, those in the record room are nameless; yet many of them know who we are, what we do, and how we behave. Undoubtedly, they resent our brusqueness and, I am sure, our high incomes compared to theirs. They would be even more upset if they could identify the occasional surgeon who dictates an operative note in such a way as to make the insurance company believe he deserves a high fee for a procedure he pretends was more complex than it was.

The fact that an operative note or a discharge summary is detailed does not necessarily make it true. Some doctors are so adept at covering their tracks that, should a complication occur, the record would not reveal an error or lapse. These physicians, though shrewd, are usually not the best. Although they are masters of connivery, their success is usually limited and brittle; they cannot relax because they do not want others to know their game—but more are onto it than they realize.

During my residency, it was customary to dictate into the operative note not only what one did during the procedure but also what one would have done if the operation were to take place again; for example, a different incision or closure. Then, the operative note was considered a learning experience as well as a record. Today, however, that type of self-exposure would make a malpractice attorney salivate. From time to time, record rooms in other hospitals have unwittingly hired people who have come to spy. These undercover agents have obtained information damaging to the hospital and individual doctors and, sometimes, to patients. In some instances, we must admit that hospitals and physicians have not been competent and honest, and that the ready availability of plaintiff attorneys has resulted in just compensation and has even improved medical care.

The record room is vulnerable also to the computer on which it totally depends. Increasing access threatens patient confidentiality. Today one can obtain with little effort much that should remain private.

I am now taking the time to read a discharge summary of a recent patient. It begins in the usual fashion: "This was the first Beth Israel Hospital admission for this 47-year-old married housewife who was admitted for revision of facial scars sustained in an auto accident three years ago." Like the dog in the Sherlock Holmes story who did not bark in the night, that sentence is noteworthy for what it did not say. Mrs. Amy Wright, petite, vivacious, and attractive, like an aging cheerleader, was returning from a tryst when her car skidded. She was driving too fast for that wintry day, and she said, "I knew that I should have left earlier." Her husband, a sales representative, obligingly was out of town. She had told me these circumstances without prefacing them with a plea for secrecy. I appreciated that she realized I would not divulge such information. Although her affair had been long-standing, she terminated it shortly afterward.

"I think I will stay at home. After all, my face can't stand many more scars."

A previous operation had improved the scars, and this recent procedure did a little more for her; yet her scarring is permanent. I wonder whether, when she applies makeup, she thinks of her accident. I wonder also whether she has told her husband, with whom I have never even spoken. If I did meet him, I would feel uncomfortable, knowing about his wife's infidelity, of which he might be unaware. Patient confidentiality sometimes becomes physician complicity. The inconsistency is that, while I deplore electronic invasion of patients' privacy, I am unhappy in maintaining it for Amy. My unease is due to empathizing with her husband while sympathizing with her.

Thoughts of Amy Wright give way to the reality of my schedule today. Before I go to the office, I still have to see Louise Brewster, who was admitted to the hospital yesterday. This preoperative visit is important because it is an opportunity for her to ask more questions and for me to continue planning her operation. This afternoon I will reconstruct her right breast, removed because of cancer.

Miss Brewster is watching the news, waiting for me. She is sitting in bed, wearing makeup and a blue bathrobe studded with pink rosebuds. Underneath she has capitulated to the system and has on the usual hospital gown, drab and dehumanizing. My recurring thought is why someone has not designed a hospital gown that is chic as well as practical.

Miss Brewster, at forty-five, looks her age. She is attractive despite her aquiline nose. Her hair is short and dark brown, and her eyes active and intelligent. She smiles easily and frequently nods in assent. She is a legal secretary and seems always prepared, in charge of the moment. Precision and organization are her allies and aid her composure. She is the kind of patient who arrives punctually, with a sheet of questions, and makes notes during the consultation. Yet she does this with grace, without apparent anxiety, without burying her nose in her pad of paper. Unmarried, she lives alone in Boston. She is emotionally close to her parents, a distinguished elderly couple, who are in a nearby town and came with her the first time she saw me. Two years before Miss Brewster consulted me, she had lost her right breast to cancer, but because the malignancy had spread to her axillary nodes, she underwent six months of chemotherapy and four months of radiation. Now, without signs of recurrence, she, with the support of her general surgeon, wants breast reconstruction.

A few years ago, encouragement from the doctor who did the mastectomy was usually withheld or given reluctantly. It is different today: women do not have to beg or convince their surgeon in order to regain what their disease and their operation have taken from them.

As Miss Brewster was leaving the office after her consultation—her parents had already gone out the door—she asked whether she could return for another discussion. I, of course, agreed. When she saw me again, she was with a male friend, a tall slender man, thinning hair, in his mid-fifties. They had met, Miss Brewster later told me, when he had worked in a bank near her office. For several years they had been intimate although he was married. After his divorce they were to be husband and wife. Unfortunately, she then developed breast cancer. Whether the marriage had been postponed or now would never take place, I did not know. He was quiet, although when he talked, his voice had a memorable, resonant quality. He was attentive and supportive, but I had the impression that he was disengaging gently since he never spoke of them as being together in the future. He never said "we." Perhaps, now that he had his freedom, he did not want to lose it to somebody else's cancer.

I have known Louise Brewster only since she had cancer and her mastectomy. As her surgeon, I have the peculiar sensation of being both a viewer and a participant in the movie of her life. With her and with many of my patients, I have the futile urge to send for the first reel, to see what she was like when she started kindergarten, when she had her sixteenth birthday party, and when she went on her first date. What youngster can possibly imagine herself unmarried with one breast, fighting cancer at mid-life? As a physician, I am ever mindful that in our society, which owes so much to science, chance still is an important determinant of our lives. My Uncle Charlie used to say, "Life can do a hell of a job on some people." The zealots of dieting and jogging are like ants scurrying under the foot of fate. Anyone who is in the medical arena knows how unfair life can be; it is a giant dart game without rules and the human being as the target. Plastic surgery attempts to right the balance, by taking from a burdened person his or her deformity, congenital or acquired, capriciously imposed.

We are probably the only animals who persistently ask why. In fact, Miss Brewster made a point of telling me that she had been surprised by her cancer because nobody in her family had it. She seemed bewildered, since there was no explanation for her misfortune. It was the old question: "Why me?" But with her, it was also "Why now?" She had some guilt, I sensed, about having some part in the dissolution of a marriage, and I am sure that she was thinking more than was healthy for her about divine retribution. Cancer is an unfailing inducer of primitive thoughts.

When I had discussed her operation with the medical student assigned to us, he doubted the wisdom of reconstructing her breast, since the tumor had already spread to her axillary lymph nodes, significantly decreasing her chances of survival, despite her subsequent radiation and chemotherapy.

The medical student, whom I know as a compassionate doctor-to-be, had asked the question that we plastic surgeons must often answer, especially in these days of increased consciousness over rising hospital costs. My reply was that determining whom to treat and whom to refuse was fortunately beyond most doctors' job requirements. I, for one, lack the knowledge and wisdom and perhaps even the right, except in an emergency, to decide who has priority for my ministrations. Since every human must die, even doctors, one could argue that it is futile ever to exert oneself therapeutically. To take an absurd position, why operate on a child who at best will eventually die as an old man? Why should we treat those terminally ill from cancer? The modus operandi of every physician is that he or she should function to the best of his or her ability in the interest of the patient at a particular time in the life of that patient and that doctor.

I remember another patient who had a mastectomy but whose cancer later metastasized widely. She no longer responded to chemotherapy and was slowly weakening, but she wanted a breast reconstruction.

"I want to be a woman when I meet God," she said.

After much discussion with her husband, her pastor, and her other doctors—all of whom supported her and me—I did the procedure, and six months later she died. In her final weeks, she continued to do many things. The ordinary tasks became the extraordinary: getting up in the morning, showering, dressing, caring for her house, her children, and her husband; spending time with her friends, even having dinner parties, writing letters against nuclear armament, volunteering at church; taking pleasure when she could despite her physical and emotional pain. Would that most of us who are well could do what she did when she was dying! The time I gave her I still consider well spent.

Recently a colleague replanted a hand that a suicidal patient had sawed off. Six weeks later, the patient successfully took his own life. Was it a mistake and a waste for my friend and the team of doctors and nurses to make the effort for this person in such a lengthy, complicated procedure? I think not. While I can understand someone's having an opposite viewpoint, I would not want him or her to be my physician. Maybe my opinion will change if and when I am an octogenarian wanting to die peacefully with the memory of what I used to be.

For most plastic surgeons, the quality of the patient's life is a central concern. That is what brought Miss Brewster to me. In her own words, she said that she wanted to "feel better" about herself and not to look down and appear "deformed and one-sided." That does not seem too much to ask, since it is what I would like for my family or myself: for life to be good as well as long, and if it cannot be long, at least as good as possible.

From a technical standpoint, Miss Brewster has one advantage with regard to reconstruction: her opposite breast is small. If her other breast were large and pendulous, it would be harder to achieve a good match without reducing the remaining breast. Miss Brewster requires only one operation, the so-called latissimus dorsi musculocutaneous flap, using the muscle and skin of her back. This will serve as tissue for making a new left breast. The tradeoff will be a scar on the back, but I can place it in the line of her bra. Using the abdomen as a donor site was another alternative that we had discussed, but Miss Brewster had objected to having an abdominal scar. Her male friend made it clear that the decision was hers.

In order to do the operation properly, I go into her room now to mark her out, to draw with a skin pencil the dimensions of the proposed flap. The residents have already made their rounds, and I prefer seeing her alone since it would embarrass her to be naked in front of a group while I put lines on her. After the usual greetings, I ask, "Would you mind if I measured you now? It is not possible to do it in the operating room when you are lying down and asleep. Do you have panties on?"

No matter how I phrase the last question, it never glides by easily. Because of my own modesty, I am mindful how disconcerting it is to stand nude or scantily dressed before someone in a medical situation. When the observer is of the opposite sex, being minimally clad is even more disagreeable. When I was a second-year medical student, the initial session of our course in physical diagnosis was given by a very elegant surgeon, the type who marries rich. "Gentlemen," he said, "what I am going to show you now is how to prepare a woman for examination." We then went to a lady's bedside, and he deftly examined her by using a towel that, like a toreador, he moved up and down, blocking out the parts he was not actually touching. Through the mobile window, he did a thorough examination without upsetting the patient, who was in her early twenties.

Later, in that same course, I witnessed a demonstration with an opposite intent. My instructor, visiting from England, had given me a patient who, he had been told, "would be good for the students," still a favorite expression in teaching hospitals. The patient was a far from congenial fifty-year-old executive. "Why should I be examined by you, a medical student?" he asked. He answered his own question as I would have done had I the courage. "So you can learn, eh? Well, learn somewhere else."

I crawled away, defeated, demeaned. My mentor, however, sensed a rare pedagogical opportunity. What he did then, in 1953, he could not and probably would not do today. He led us four students into the patient's room and said, "Ah, Mr. Winston, so good of you to see us. I have brought a few medical students with me to check some things on you. Stand right up and get undressed, completely." The formidable tycoon became a dutiful employee who without a word permitted a total examination, including a rectal from all of us. After we had left, my instructor said, "Goldwyn, never forget that, when any patient gives you a difficult time, get him undressed. A naked patient is much more manageable." It is true, of course. If we could force the leaders of every nuclear nation to divest their clothing before making hostile speeches, we would probably have world peace within a week. Occasionally when someone vexes me verbally, I imagine him or her without clothes. It does wonders for one's stability.

How we would deal with female nudity, especially in a professional setting, was an early anxiety for most of us males entering medical school. True, we had fumbled and tumbled in the dark with a woman on occasion. Except for a few of us who were married, we had never lived with a woman. Mothers and sisters did not count. Immediately after registration, many classmates enrolled in a live model drawing class at the nearby Museum of Fine Arts. Others, like me, to get pre-battle experience, went to watch a birth.

Now, in Miss Brewster's room, thirty years after medical school, I am again with someone half-dressed; this time I am older by twenty years than was my surgical instructor and I am ten years senior to my patient. As I am drawing on her, I tell her a story to relax her and, I confess, myself also. A couple of years ago, I was doing the same thing when a student nurse whom I did not know walked into the room, then fled to tell the head nurse, "There is a man in a suit drawing on a naked patient." The head nurse ran back, looked, and said, "That's only Dr. Goldwyn." I felt like the family idiot who causes a commotion when he unexpectedly wanders from his room to meet company downstairs and then has to be explained away.

My patient laughs; we both enjoy the change in our peripheral resistance. I can see her shoulders and abdominal muscles relax. No more the West Point pose.

"Please don't wash these markings off in the shower," I say.

"I showered last night."

I then repeat certain aspects of the procedure, points that we had discussed in her previous visits to my office. Repetition is good not just for medical-legal purposes but also because it lessens the anxiety, since the patient becomes more familiar with what will soon happen.

Many surgeons unfortunately prolong their procedures because they do their thinking at the time of operation, when they should have done much of it before.

The operating room staff, other surgeons, and all patients must endure the effects of another disease peculiar to surgeons, underestimating the length of an operation. In scheduling their cases, most surgeons say that they will finish a cholecystectomy, for example, in less time than it will actually take. Speed is usually valued for itself, and most surgeons like to think that they can do a procedure quickly. This fault, I believe, is genetic since it constitutes part of a syndrome characterized also by underestimating blood loss, overestimating the number of procedures performed, and minimizing complications. This kind of person is also likely to say that he lives just twenty minutes away from the hospital, when it is in reality a forty-minute drive. The delusion is minor and harmless, designed to convince himself and others that he has the world to his liking and has made all the correct decisions in his life.

Sometimes, the surgeon's self-deception, however, poses a problem to the patient and ultimately to the surgeon as well. Surgeons consistently underrate the pain that a patient will have. Since they believe in the operations they perform and tend to be optimistic, they unwittingly avoid some of the negative aspects. Some surgeons, for instance, think they are painless operators. If the patient has severe discomfort postoperatively, the surgeon unconsciously may consider it an affront to his skill and may withhold pain relief.

In the past, many patients were poorly informed about an operation, not because the surgeon was a deceiver but because he was a denier. He was happy to continue being oblivious to the rigors and risks of surgery. Occasionally aiding him in this misapprehension is the patient, who may not want to hear what could go wrong and so does not ask questions or seek explanations.

"How long will the operation last?" Miss Brewster now asks me.

"About three and a half hours," I reply. Purposely I said "about three and a half hours," instead of three or four hours, so that she will feel more confident with this precision. As a matter of fact, it is the usual length of time for this operation.

"Whom do you wish me to call after it is over, to let them know you did well?" I ask.

"My parents," she replies.

"Anyone else?" We both know what I mean, and she smiles.

"Would it be too much?"

"Of course not."

I remind Miss Brewster not to eat or drink anything in the event that someone mistakenly brings her a breakfast tray. Any patient having general anesthesia, even extensive local anesthesia, should not eat or drink for at least eight hours prior to operation. A patient with a full stomach runs the danger of vomiting and aspirating.

As I get ready to leave, I put my hand on her shoulder and say, "Things will go very well."

She replies, "I have every confidence in you. I am glad you are my surgeon, but I still wish you good luck."

Many patients say "good luck" to their surgeon. It is an obeisance to the reign of chance, an acknowledgment of ultimate helplessness for both the patient and the surgeon. If I said "good luck" to Miss Brewster, I would be guilty of a tactical error that would increase her anxiety. It is better for the patient to recognize uncertainty rather than have the surgeon emphasize it so close to operation. In the consultations preceding the operation, the surgeon has a duty to talk about undesirable happenings beyond his or her control. Now is not the occasion for repeating the doleful litany.

Nor is it appropriate to reply to Miss Brewster as a colleague once did to his patient, "You and I don't really need luck. I've planned everything to the nth degree." It is perplexing that so many physicians are devoid of the humility that should come to them as a result of their medical failures. So powerful are their narcissism and denial that they remember only their successes. These physicians may loom large within the hospital, but they become lilliputs in the street, just a few hundred yards away, where most people would fail to recognize them.

I say "thank you" to Miss Brewster. The next time I see her, she will be helpless and I will have the power, but for both of us the outcome will still be in the laps of the gods.

I leave her room, take the elevator to the garage, and get in my car to drive to my office.

chapter 2

Conveniently, my office is just a few blocks away from the hospital. It is in a large white stone building, which has about eighty tenants, all medical. Though built at the beginning of World War I, it looks Victorian. The once-splendid apartments, the interiors of which can be seen in old photographs in the entry, have long since become offices. These suites, in the words of a patient from New York, are "typically Boston." Large but not lavish, they are traditional and solid, with an air of dependability.

Eleven hundred and one Beacon Street is a well-known medical address in Boston, easily reached by the subway line in front. At one time, about fifty years ago, the Yankee owners of the building did not rent to Jews. As far as I know, no black or Oriental tenant ever penetrated, but there were a couple of elderly female physicians when I first arrived. World War II and the migration of doctors to the military created empty offices, which caused a change in renting policies. A few Jews then trickled in.

The landlord, who was allegedly the largest taxpayer in Brookline, may have had his prejudices but he was fair in his rent. He was also careful about his clientele. While he may not have welcomed minorities, he was even more hostile to charlatans. Every renter received information about a prospective lessee, including educational background, postgraduate training, hospital affiliations, and sponsors. Finally, there was the box to check. Do you approve: yes or no? I do not remember voting against any applicant, since they all had good training and excellent recommendations. One of my fellow tenants, now retired, was Dr. William Murphy, who with Drs. Whipple and Minot won the Nobel Prize in 1934 for the successful treatment of pernicious anemia. One could recognize his patients, regal octogenarians who came for their vitamin B-12 injections.

When I opened my office, the building had ancient elevators of glacial velocity servicing the eight floors. They were run by what would now be called Uncle Tom blacks. One of them in his seventies had retired from his elevator job at Sears, Roebuck after having been there a half-century. He had found to his surprise that he had become extremely wealthy because, during his many years of service, he had taken part of his salary in stocks, which had split and accumulated prodigiously. Yet he must have missed the up-and-down routine at Sears, because he resumed his former occupation in our building. He had complained to me that the main elevator was faulty, and two weeks later its defective door injured his leg seriously. That the elevator had earned a recent certificate of safety increased my cynicism about the American shibboleth of "justice for all."

I began my practice on July 4, 1963. This association gives my country's birthday a special meaning for me. I have been in the same office for two decades. My parents generously financed the renovations and decorating and also the first few months' rent. The money was a gift, not a loan. Their philosophy, and mine, is: give to children when they need it and can enjoy it. Why wait until you die to see their happiness and to feel your usefulness? A few thousand dollars to a thirty-three-year-old means far more than a larger sum when that son or daughter is sixty.

My parents brought a bottle of champagne, and understandably they were proud and glad that finally I was a practicing surgeon after the long process of four years of college, four more of medical school, five years of general surgical residency, and two additional years of plastic surgical training.

When I became a plastic surgeon, the best residencies in plastic surgery demanded five years of general surgical training. Now the situation has changed somewhat. Trainees get into the plastic surgical lane from various routes. Although full training in general surgery is still highly desirable for entering top plastic surgical programs, other alternatives exist, such as board eligibility in a surgical specialty like otolaryngology or orthopedics.

At the present time, the United States has approximately three and a half thousand board-certified plastic surgeons. Each year about one hundred residency programs produce about two hundred who are board-eligible and ready to begin as plastic surgeons.

Most studies of plastic surgical manpower show that our specialty is becoming crowded, particularly in the urban areas. Rural states and communities still do not have enough plastic surgeons, but the plastic surgeon who wants to do a lot of cosmetic surgery will likely shy away from such places.

I was fortunate to have been asked to return to the Peter Bent Brigham Hospital and also to receive an appointment to the staff of the Beth Israel Hospital. I became a consultant at the Robert Breck Brigham Hospital, which was then separate from the Peter Bent. Situated on a hill, the Robert Breck Brigham Hospital was a graceful, somewhat archaic structure, where patients with collagen diseases, especially arthritis, received singular care. The nurses, many of whom came from Ireland, were laudably attentive to patients and respectful to doctors. Going there to see patients with leg ulcers and other problems gave me a pleasant sensation of slipping back in time. I was grateful for that tranquil interlude. The pace of the hospital was salubrious and slow, befitting the type of progress that patients could expect to make. They did not feel embarrassed or left behind, as they would in a hectic hospital devoted primarily to acute care.

In those early years of practice, I operated regularly as well at the West Roxbury Veterans' Administration Hospital. There I was consultant in plastic surgery to general surgical patients and to those on the spinal cord injury service. In addition, once a month, I drove forty miles west to the Burbank Hospital in Fitchburg, where there was no plastic surgeon. I had a large outpatient clinic there and also operated on three to six patients in the course of a very long day.

When I began practice, I was the seventeenth board-eligible plastic surgeon in Massachusetts; there are now more than seventy-five. In those days, I did not have to create a need for myself; I was needed, and people were grateful for whatever skills I had. Professional success came quickly.

The other day, I heard an attorney in his thirties ask a colleague of apparently the same age how his life was going.

"I am in the home stretch of a mediocre career," he replied.

Although he laughed, he might have been serious.

My former chief of plastic surgery in Pittsburgh would remind us residents: "If you aim at nothing, you generally will hit the mark."

To a young resident planning a career in plastic surgery, I would still say that he will have a good future if he works hard, with intelligence and imagination, and is lucky with his health. But if he views plastic surgery primarily as a good way of making a living, he will probably have a less than fulfilling life and his patients will receive uninspired care.

Even if he is highly skilled and properly motivated, the practice of plastic surgery will be different from what it was for me and my contemporaries. The economics of a medical career are not what they were. So great is the current cost of education that this resident has probably already accumulated a significant debt after four years of college and four years of medical school. He will be behind an even more massive financial eight ball after another six to seven years of residency.

The proliferation of plastic surgeons has created a marketplace that is more competitive than it was when I began practice. The new plastic surgeon will have little chance of being the only plastic surgeon around.

He will be doing more to earn less than those of my generation. Many laws recently enacted will recompense physicians with lower fixed fees than they used to get, without permitting them to bill the patient for the difference between what they request from the insurance company and what they receive. Their incomes will be relatively less than what they would have been twenty years ago. Today, unlike then, we in medicine also have to contend with the reality of malpractice suits and the crunch of malpractice insurance.

I remember clearly the first person I saw in practice. My office door had been opened officially for no more than two hours when an elderly patient wandered in. My secretary and I greeted him as if he were walking manna. How had he heard of me? I asked myself. The truth was that he hadn't. He was almost blind and thought that he was in the office of the ophthalmologist who was directly opposite. But, within the first week of practice, I did have a patient of my own. Mrs. Jo Welch was a very well-dressed, middle-aged woman, referred because she had fallen on her yacht and had struck her cheek, sustaining a depressed fracture of the underlying bone. She had gone to another doctor, but she did not have confidence in him. Looking around my office, the furnishings of which are the same today, she obviously liked not only its look of authority but also the feeling of being in a comfortable living room. Its lived-in appearance and its air of solidity worked, I am sure, in my favor.

"I am glad I found you because you obviously have had the experience to deal with this," she said. While it was true I did have the experience, it had come from my residency, not my practice. One learns quickly the wisdom of silence. Fortunately, her operation went well, and she subsequently sent me many of her friends for elective surgery.

I was lucky in another respect: no disasters occurred early in my professional life. While I had the usual complications, as does any surgeon—I was honest enough to admit them—I did not experience a catastrophe. One young doctor, just in practice, was removing a wart on the finger of his partner's twelve-year-old son, when the patient reacted adversely to the local anesthetic and died from cardiac arrest. That luckless surgeon moved to another state.

In my own instance, with time, the reality of *being* established caught up with my early image of *looking* established, an adjective from another generation, that of my parents. Some of their friends would boast of having a son or nephew who not only was a doctor but was also a "diagnostician." Most likely the person described was an internist, but I pictured a doctor with a massive head, who just diagnosed, never treated. He was too important for that. Maybe he would say only "diabetes mellitus" and then wearily ask his secretary to call the next patient.

How patients select their doctor would be an engrossing study. One of my early patients told me that he got my name from someone leaving the building with a "beautiful dressing" on his neck. He followed him, even into the trolley, and asked who had done the dressing because he had a "lump" on his neck and would probably require the same operation. How many patients came to me because of my dressings, I did not know, but I would hope that most came because of my other skills.

What the first few years in practice lacked in revenue,

they made up for in comedy. Two unusual incidents occurred because of my business cards.

The first involved an elderly male, whom I saw because of a skin cancer of his face. He had a lesion that merited excision. At the time of operation, he told me that I had really impressed him.

"You are so young to be so successful. You must have a lot of energy, going back and forth between Boston and Miami," he said.

"What do you mean?" I asked, since I had not been to Miami for at least five years.

"Well, you have an office in Miami," he replied, looking confused.

"I do?" I asked.

"Well, that's what your card says."

He showed me a card that my secretary had given him. In fact, he was correct. A printing error had my name, but a Miami address. Somehow, my cards and those of another surgeon had become mixed up. By throwing away a few other misprinted cards, I closed my Miami office.

The second odd event was on the night that my wife and I talked to a man who had been sent by our temple to sell us cemetery plots. Complying with the inevitable, we purchased four: land that I futilely hope will go forever unused. The elderly purveyor of life's essentials left me his card.

During the night, I had an emergency, an eleven-year-old boy with a dog bite. After I repaired it in the emergency room, I told the father to make an appointment for his son in five days at my office, where I would remove the stitches.

"Do you have a card?" the father asked.

"Certainly," I replied.

I handed him a card.

The boy's father looked at it and said, "You doctors got it all figured out. If you make a mistake, someone will bury it for you." I was perplexed until he showed me the card that I had given to him. It belonged to the cemetery plot salesman.

Fortunately, now I do not yearn for patients. More call for appointments than I can quickly accommodate. With that gain, however, I have lost unfilled hours, about which I used to complain. There came a point, about three years after I started practice, when I tried to fit in as soon as possible everybody who called. I had not yet learned to say "no," still a rare response for me. Feeling oppressed by my schedule, and desiring to become less clock conscious, I stopped wearing a watch and still don't. This gesture has been more symbolic than effectual; it was not even original, since my chief in Pittsburgh, Dr. White, allegedly had cast his very expensive watch into the confluence of the Monongahela and Allegheny rivers. Somehow the way he did it, from a lofty height, seemed more disdainful than my winging my timepiece into the Charles River as I stood on its level, littered bank.

With regard to time, my Greenwich points are when I must first be in the office and when I must next be in the operating room; all else fits in between. Any success in scheduling is due to the validity of the inverse of Parkinson's Law: Tasks will accommodate to the time available. For a plastic surgeon and his patients, there is another law. More patients mean more operations. How well I recall my conversation with one of the senior plastic surgeons in town. We were in the plastic surgical clinic at the hospital when he excused himself because he had to begin the first of five nasal operations. Because I had been in practice only six months, his pronouncement was awesome. I spoke the truth, "I hope someday I can have a practice like yours." He looked at me thoughtfully and replied, "It is hard for you to understand now, but I wish that I had a schedule like yours."

For those who are clinical surgeons, not doing primarily research, there is no moderation. We are always working to the limit and slightly beyond. The golden mean may exist in theory, but in practice we are unable to find it or, if we do, to keep it for long. Because our energies and ambition tend to maximize, we stretch ourselves beyond our elastic limit. The psychiatrist has a built in regulator, one patient per hour, at least according to the traditional schedule. He or she can elongate the working day but only so far. Even a crazy patient would think it odd to be seen at eleven at night or three in the morning, but a surgeon is a fitter-inner. Despite my protestations and attempts not to be, I keep loading my pack, to the consternation of my secretaries. I usually arrive at the office before they do, and before my patients, whose appointments begin around eight o'clock on Mondays and Wednesdays and later in the morning on Fridays. One of my quirks is that I like to be ready for them. If a patient arrives very early and is waiting for me, I become unnecessarily irritated, feeling that I shall be pounced upon, as if by lurking lions ready to devour me. When I am fatigued, a line blurs between my being pleased to extend myself for patients and my being fearful that I shall be used up. I hear myself saying, reproachfully, "You certainly are here early." The patient senses my displeasure, which fortunately for us both is only momentary; nevertheless, I feel guilty. Usually the first patient of the day is known to me and will be able to slip this negative experience into what hopefully have been other positive encounters. Is this patient an unwitting target of my displeasure at having to begin work? I doubt it, since I do not react this way at the hospital when I see my preoperative patients. As I have analyzed it, it is a question of control. Being compulsive in my work, I need to have everything in order, and a patient getting to my office before I do is decidedly out of order.

This morning no one is waiting for me when I enter my office suite. Neither the building nor my office has changed much since I began practice. The original decor is still evident. I furnished my office to be comfortable for me, not to impress patients of any particular stratum. I do not wish either to lure or to offend through my office, which is tranquil and homey: relaxing chairs and sofa, walnut paneling, a Cheret poster, my daughters' earliest drawings, knickknacks from family trips abroad.

One of my colleagues told me that he designed his office to be elegant so that the rich will be at ease. That the "poor need not apply for help" runs counter to my concept of a doctor and his office. In general, those who do aesthetic surgery have the most elaborate offices and certainly the least number of patients on Medicaid. They know that someone who wants to look chic and youthful would avoid a drab and gloomy office. Those doctors are untroubled in the marketplace of the twentieth century and actually may enjoy it.

Erma Bombeck advised her readers against going to a doctor whose office plants are dying. So, also, I would not choose a physician whose office is dirty and whose appearance is unkempt. My personal bias is that I would also avoid a doctor who has built a mini-Versailles.

What a doctor displays for reading—and "displays" is the correct word—gives some insight into the image he or she is attempting to project. If the slant is toward the beautiful rich, it would be suicidal to have *Hot Rod* and *Baseball Digest*. The financially blessed would be comfortable with periodicals on gardening and yachting but certainly not those on home repairs. In my office, I am selfish enough to have primarily what I like to read and then hope it will satisfy most of my patients: *Time, Architectural Design, Art in America, Science, Boston Magazine*. My secretaries have added *People,* whose fast disappearance from the waiting room attests to the popularity of gossip.

An office is part of making a living, a process that requires selling ourselves to some degree, or at least presenting ourselves favorably enough so we and our props do not become obstacles to the person seeking our services. How we physicians do this without squandering our essence is the difficult task.

I go through my usual procedure of turning on the lights, changing into a white coat that is similar to the ones I wore as a resident and getting out my camera. I am ready for Alicia Wells, whose footsteps I hear in the hallway. This is a good way to start my office day, I muse. Although Alicia is beautiful—an ordinary word for an unusual condition—other adjectives come to mind: refined, elegant, cultured, tall, graceful, the type of woman that would make even the quintessential boor rise as she entered a room.

She brings out the sensual maleness in me. A respected editor in an old Boston publishing house, she has come to see me for the past four years because she is afraid of aging. To be specific, she does not mind getting older as much as looking older. Now forty, she once told me what her mother had said to her: "A beautiful woman dies twice."

Alicia looks like her mother, whose picture she once showed me. She remembered how her mother "suddenly aged" and, five years ago, withered away in a nursing home—or what my Chinese guide in Peking called "a prison for parents."

Every year I inspect Alicia's face for the lines and sagging that she says have become worse. For comparison, we look at the photographs taken on her last visit. Her appointment is always in May, the month in her life when, she says, "All the bad things happen." She mentions her mother's death as an example and "other events like that," without specifying.

There is a man somewhere, I know. I fantasize that it is someone married (naturally, like me). I envy him not just for what I assume, perhaps wrongly, must be physical ecstasy but the knowledge he must have of her being. Alicia has a reticence that borders on the mysterious. The English poet was correct: "A veiled beauty, like an eclipse, gathers the most observers."

She is fighting hard not to become yesterday's woman. She would concur with what one of my patients said: "I don't ever want to get to the stage where I see my face melting like wax."

Alicia and her mirror spend a lot of time together. And she probably cannot joke about it, as did Tallulah Bankhead: "Darling, they're not making mirrors the way they used to."

For Alicia, appearance is central to her being. For most

of us, how we look is important, but we are reluctant to admit how often we think of our physical features. I am not sure how dealing with the appearance of others has affected my preoccupation with my own looks. Detailed self-scrutiny I reserve for weekends. The rest of the time I am too rushed and too fearful to take careful stock.

Beauty is undemocratic. Not everyone has it or can get it, even with the aid of a phalanx of plastic surgeons. While most intellectuals are ready to reward scholarly achievement and praise character, they are reluctant to glorify human pulchritude, which is usually due to an accident of birth. Yet these same individuals would like to be considered at least attractive and would despise anyone who called their children ugly. Their senses quicken in the presence of someone who to them is beautiful, and they are not loath to laud a beautiful flower, sunset, or painting. This calls to mind what Wolinski, the French humorist, said about willingly giving up the "sight of all the sunsets of Venice for that of a woman's bottom."

Despite the Puritan ethic, which does not worship physical beauty, males in Boston, even Brahmins, still turn their head in reverence and expectation when a pretty woman passes. And women notice a good-looking man, but they are more controlled in their public reactions.

Every society and culture, and even the more complex animals (note I avoided "higher") on the evolutionary scale, have their own rating index for physical attributes. It is unambiguous to a particular animal species or group of human beings who among them most clearly fulfills their criteria of physical perfection. I have never heard a satisfying explanation for this phenomenon, the ranking of beauty (or the converse, of ugliness) within a culture or subculture. Darwin thought it related to maintenance of the species: mating between those supposedly without physical defects would result in healthier offspring.

Numerous psychological studies have shown that subjects rate those who are better looking as being more intelligent. Those less attractive physically are victims of the tyranny of the beautiful.

The Swami Prabhupada told a story to put beauty in what he considered its proper place. He described a girl of singular looks and character who wanted to teach an insistent suitor a lesson about absolute beauty and truth. She instructed him to return in a week, during which she took purgatives and laxatives. She stored her vomit and stool in pots. When the expectant man returned, he saw only an ugly, emaciated woman, whom he asked the whereabouts of the beautiful woman. After she then disclosed her identity, he refused to believe her until she showed him the ingredients of her beauty in the foul-smelling containers.

The man and woman in this story never married, as one might suspect. Do those who mate with persons others would consider devastatingly ugly attempt to grasp life at its core, or are they simply poor choosers?

In my practice, I have noted that some men who are married to eminently unattractive women enjoy their physical superiority. These men seem to take pleasure in having a beholden woman, grateful for their attention. If the wife decides, perhaps as a result of psychotherapy, to improve her looks, the husband usually objects. My surgery may release his slave.

If Alicia Wells, now in my office, is a slave, it is not because of ugliness. It is because of her beauty, her commitment to preserving it. Nevertheless, she has not reached the point where she has proclaimed, as did another patient: "Moisturizer is my religion."

We frequently say that "Beauty is in the eye of the beholder." The beholder may be the person himself or herself. I have had many patients whom everyone would judge to be beautiful but who, nevertheless, consider themselves the opposite. In most instances, it was a competitive mother who undermined her child's self-esteem. Initially, my reaction was to get angry at the mother in absentia. This was wrong, because I did not have the facts. Moreover, it is not my function to take sides. Far better for me to listen. My behavior was a tactical error from another standpoint: it awakened anger in my patient toward her mother and increased her guilt.

For Alicia Wells, today, the rituals remain the same: taking pictures, showing her slides from the last visit. I observe her in her self-scrutiny, as she holds the mirror, turning it slowly from side to side. At home she must have a full-length mirror—more body to scrutinize, to defend against the advance of aging. But aging is a war with a long front, and it ceases only with death. Although I might be able to help her against future depredations on her face, breasts, abdomen, and even thighs, I cannot renovate everything. Her hands, for example, will give her away, even if I go to the extreme of excising extra skin and lightening the aging spots with a chemical peel. The gloved Victorians knew what they were doing. The less that is exposed, the less there is to find wanting.

With Alicia, this year, as before, the sagging and wrinkling are too minimal for surgery. She sighs but does not seem surprised. As she leaves the examining room, I tell her to call my secretary to get a "date" for next year.

I then realize that I said "date" instead of "appointment." I hope she did not catch my slip, but I sense she did because of the way she smiles.

In plastic surgery, the ratio of those who come for consultation to those who have an operation is high. Unlike Alicia Wells, most patients make an appointment to obtain an operation and are disappointed if you do not agree to it. Because of the increase in hospital costs and competition for available operating time, many plastic surgeons have built their own surgical facilities. I have not done so for several reasons. My office presently would not safely accommodate these arrangements; I would probably have to move. Furthermore, I wish to operate in a teaching hospital, where I believe I have the duty to instruct residents as well as colleagues in what plastic surgery can do. As clinical professor of surgery at Harvard Medical School, I would like my specialty to have influence and to have impact on patient care as well as on the future careers of students and residents. Being in my office more, though it would be convenient, would not achieve these objectives.

The operations that plastic surgeons perform in their offices are almost always cosmetic procedures, which insurance companies do not finance. Since the patient must pay those expenses, one does him a favor by reducing hospital costs. Nevertheless, I have observed that many surgeons in their own operating facilities increase their fees substantially so that, even if they charge less for their operating room, the total bill is the same or more than their colleagues who operate at hospitals. An additional fact for the surgeon to consider is that having one's own operating room requires personnel who must be paid, even when no work is in progress.

Access to an operating room away from a university does have another advantage, however. Some surgeons can hide the fact that they are doing cosmetic surgery. Even a decade ago at most medical schools, especially those in the Northeast, a surgeon performing an aesthetic operation was not regarded highly by his colleagues. He was doing trivial surgery, operations designed to make money and to indulge the rich and self-centered. The chief of surgery, almost always a general surgeon up to his waist in viscera, considered the eyelidplasty or facelift the surgical equivalent of a beauty salon permanent wave. To medical officialdom, the plastic surgeon was an expensive beautician, a view that is not unknown today. In fact, when I was visiting the late Dr. John Converse at Bellevue in New York City, this internationally honored plastic surgeon told me he never wanted more than two cosmetic procedures scheduled a day on his service, since it would be harmful to the image of his department's standing within the hospital. For that reason, he said, he and his associates used another hospital for most of their aesthetic work.

As a member of a minority, I can understand the pressure they felt to maintain appearances and the discomfort they experienced in their professional isolation. For emotional and career survival, many plastic surgeons of the past generation adopted the prejudices of those in power who were not plastic surgeons. They, too, decried and denigrated cosmetic surgery, which is an intrinsic part of plastic surgery. For them, it had been hard enough selling reconstructive surgery to the rest of medicine and surgery, let alone cosmetic procedures. The surgery of appearance is still beyond the pale to many physicians, except when they have personal need of it. Even now many plastic surgeons wrestle with what they perceive is the dichotomy between the cosmetic and reconstructive elements within our field. Some feel tainted by cosmetic surgery; yet many who profess such a thought engage in it, sometimes secretly, outside the university hospital. Aesthetic surgery historically became like masturbation, practiced but not acknowledged.

When the American Society for Aesthetic Plastic Surgery was founded, there was opposition. Many believed that the American Society of Plastic and Reconstructive Surgeons, Inc., to which most American plastic surgeons belong, was sufficient to answer their needs. The further implication of that position was that every plastic surgeon should be able to do aesthetic surgery. The fact is that not every plastic surgeon can do it properly and not everyone wishes to do it at all. Many plastic surgeons viewed this new Aesthetic Society as harming needlessly an already small specialty by further subdividing it. Not surprisingly, some of those critics later joined it. As a member of the American Society for Aesthetic Plastic Surgery, I am uncomfortably conscious that the spelling of "aesthetic" with the "a" is perhaps not just a matter of preferred usage but an unconscious attempt to elevate status by emphasizing classical Greek lineage. This is more evidence, although subtle, of the lack of ease that many who do aesthetic surgery (or should it be "esthetic"?) feel; they do not like being called "cosmetic surgeons"—again the unfavorable, nonmedical connotation of a beauty parlor.

I schedule all my operations, aesthetic or not, at my university hospital. *Romanus sum*—whatever I am, I am, like it or not, as far as the rest of surgery and medicine are concerned. My professional confidence comes largely from the fact that I was a secure, valued only child. I never needed to look behind me, fearful that others would take something away from me. Since I have no conflict over what I do in my work, I can concentrate on my allegiance to the patient. Everything else becomes secondary and falls into place. This is an expression less of my magnanimity than of my self-esteem.

No matter how the individual plastic surgeon may regard himself or his work, the public equates plastic surgery more with cosmetic or aesthetic surgery than with anything else. At most parties, when people realize that I am a plastic surgeon, women in particular laugh nervously, pull back their facial skin, and usually inquire about rejuvenating operations. It is a rare white, upper middle-class woman over the age of forty who has not contemplated more than once a procedure to make herself look younger.

"I'll be calling your office soon for an appointment" is a remark said somewhat in jest. But I never reply, "Oh, you don't need it," unless I really believe it.

I am frequently asked how much of my practice is "cosmetic" and how much "reconstructive." Most plastic surgeons, even those doing only one type, find it hard to admit precise percentages since their own self-image pushes them to think that they are broader based than they probably are. Once I witnessed a plastic surgeon on the defensive because someone said, "I suppose you don't do nose jobs."

"I certainly do," he replied, even though he did mostly

hand operations and no more than one or two rhinoplasties a year. He had to defend a stereotype that he usually worked hard to avoid.

Now the public is enthralled with replantation, but not every plastic surgeon does this, certainly not most older than fifty. Putting back a leg or a finger is exciting and important, but most people cannot imagine themselves requiring that kind of care. Yet everyone can fantasize about looking younger as he or she gets older. That is why plastic surgery has become an obsession with the media, particularly women's programs and publications, even those run for and by women who have presumably been "liberated." No one likes getting older, but women try to do more about it. Of every hundred patients having an operation for aging, at least eighty-five are female. What makes this figure even more interesting is that ninety-eight percent of all plastic surgeons in the United States are male.

A significant portion of my week concerns the physical appearance of women. I spend many hours trying to preserve beauty in those who have it, to restore it to those who have lost it, and to give it, if possible, to those who may lack it. That my mother is beautiful is probably a strong factor in this aspect of my surgical commitment—I say this without benefit of psychoanalysis! That I love my mother, and even like her, takes considerable courage to admit in this era when children gain status by despising parents. With respect to myself and my work, am I symbolically forestalling my mother's decline?

The reactions of women to aging and their reasons for wanting a facelift vary. For some it is not simply to arrest the external aging process for inner gain but to retain their economic viability. As one of my older patients observed: "It's still a man's world. Most men will favor a woman who is smart, young, and attractive over someone who is fading, even if she is wiser and more experienced."

For other women, a younger male is the stimulus for surgery. A recent divorcee who detested the gathering of skin under her chin was explicit. Her lover, ten years younger than she, liked to have sex in the daylight with her on top. In that position, she thought her neck was vulnerable to scrutiny. I asked her whether he had ever said anything about it, and she replied, "No, but I have to be careful of what he may be thinking."

Alice Munro, in one of her stories, said of a woman's behavior that would seem odd to most men, "In none of this is she so exceptional. She does what women do . . ."

That women feel the need to modify their bodies to gratify themselves and others bothers me, because I have two daughters who I hope will not become overly concerned about their appearance. Yes, I make a living from what I do, but I still feel sorry on occasion for those who are under so much pressure that it pushes them to an operating room for physical renewal.

This obsession with looks begins early for women. As small girls, they are likely to identify with their mothers, who may be overly conscious of their bodies. Later, as they become young women, they are soon targets of television ads, books, and magazines that foster an insecurity about their physical being. Periodicals geared to adolescent girls have a reprehensible paucity of articles about social issues, educational opportunities, and intellectual challenges. Too little is in those pages about women who have been outstanding in the arts, sciences, and politics.

Women are being betrayed by women, who perpetuate the infantile status of the female in this society and profit from their bodily concerns. Articles that glorify the body to the exclusion of the mind affect girls and women; they affix them to the frivolous and raise their titer of tinsel. Strong language, perhaps, but let anyone doubting its truth browse through magazines such as *Self, Seventeen, Cosmopolitan,* and *McCall's.* Those groups that are active in monitoring what children in schools read should not neglect what bombards them at the corner newsstand. Perhaps journalism with a social conscience would help females at an early age to remain persons and to resist conversion to physical entities. The main message of some magazines seems to be improve your looks so that you can be wanted by a man and only then will you find fulfillment. But I cannot avoid the hard question: Am I, as a plastic surgeon, also reinforcing this situation? Reluctantly, I must answer in the affirmative. I both answer that need and create it.

chapter 3

So much has been written about the doctor-patient relationship that the phrase signals instant tedium. The physician's professional and emotional life are nevertheless in mortal danger when he or she finds the interaction with a patient boring. The patient is also at hazard from the doctor's lack of enthusiasm, which may easily degenerate into nonconcern.

What does a physician want from a patient? Cooperation and respect. Also, if we are honest, most physicians crave more than approbation; they desire gratitude. In their role as healers, doctors also want progress from their patients; they want them to get well. This last desire, of course, we and our patients cannot always satisfy.

The public correctly believes that most doctors enjoy "interesting cases"; challenges in diagnosis and treatment excite our blood. Yet, in truth, most of us would not want every patient to be beyond the norm. To have to be constantly innovative would tire and stress most of us. We take pleasure in working out a routine that is successful in treating our patients. But an occasional jolt from an unusual patient is essential to keep us alert and alive professionally. Such, indeed, was my next patient, Mrs. Adrienne Williams, whom no plastic surgeon would ever forget. What happened at the initial consultation four years ago is still with me. Then in her mid-twenties, she was noticeably tall and she moved with grace. Her luxuriant red hair framed a sensitive oval face, which was pale, despite the fact that it was in the middle of the summer. On this humid day, she had worn a loose, sheer dress that showed her pleasing figure.

Mrs. Williams was a graduate student in education and the wife of a chemical engineer. I did not know why she had come to my office. When a patient calls for an appointment, my secretaries usually ask the reason for the consultation, not to be intrusive but to schedule properly. Someone with a small skin growth, for example, usually requires less time than does a person contemplating breast reconstruction after mastectomy. Mrs. Williams said that she would discuss her problem "only with the doctor." I remember that she had trouble in stating what we in medicine call "the chief complaint." I recall also reassuring her: "Mrs. Williams, whatever problem has brought you here, I am sure I have heard before from someone who had probably sat in that very chair. Please feel free to talk to me."

Then Mrs. Williams said, after a deep breath, "I was born without a vagina." She looked at me to be sure she had not astonished me; I told her that other patients have had that same condition and I have helped them.

Evidently, the pediatrician discovered the problem when she was a girl and also that, as she said, she "did not have male parts." Some patients with absence or partial development of the vagina have gonads of the opposite sex and are hermaphrodites.

Mrs. Williams's breasts developed normally, "but I never had periods, and I do not have a uterus." This is not necessarily so in all patients lacking a normal vagina, but many have no uterus or an abnormal one.

Her father was a significant help to her in adjusting to her problem. An Iowa farmer, and someone with good psychological sense, he kept telling her he had seen this a few times in the animals on the farm, and she was "as good as anyone else." He said that she was lucky because she just had something wrong with "only one part." Her two older brothers and a younger sister also were supportive. Mrs. Williams's mother tried to be helpful but felt responsible and guilty for her daughter's plight. Going through high school, she managed well. "I made sure that with boys things never went too far." At college in Boston she met her future husband, who is "wonderful and understanding about it." She let me know that he had a congenital deformity of his hand. On both sides of the family, they were the only ones "with faulty parts," she said with a well-rehearsed line and laugh.

They had reconciled themselves to not having children. Since they came from large families, they already had a batch of nephews and nieces, to whom they were very close. As Mrs. Williams was telling me her problem, she kept looking at my face, trying to detect how I really felt about her condition. Most physicians, however, have trained themselves to remain neutral and not to react judgmentally. The ability to look blank is handy, although no physician would want to be thought without feeling.

I had to obtain some information about her sexual life. I sallied forth with "How do you and your husband manage physically," sounding like an Americanized British colonel in India. Mrs. Williams replied as if I had inquired about the kind of car they drove. "Oral sex is what we use. We both have orgasms regularly and try to have sex every night.

"I am not doing this just for my sex life, doctor. I want to be like everybody else. I feel freaky because I am different, and my husband and I spend a lot of energy trying to compensate." As I looked at Mrs. Williams on that visit, I wondered how many women passing her in the street would be jealous of her because she seemed to have everything. Most human beings envy more people than they pity, except perhaps when they go to Mexico or some other underdeveloped country. But one does not usually have to scratch very deeply to uncover somebody else's pain.

With regard to her vaginal reconstruction, although there are several procedures available, I preferred dissecting a pocket and inserting a skin graft from the buttocks as lining for the new passage. Since Mrs. Williams did have a mate, regular intercourse would be available to her, and this is necessary to thwart nature's tendency to contract tissue. Mrs. Williams told me that her vagina has remained adequate for sex.

Today's visit was to be her last since her husband had accepted a position in California. The other odd thing about Mrs. Williams was that my relationship was entirely with her. I had never seen her husband. I had spoken to him only once, and that was on the phone immediately after the operation when I told him what had transpired. Initially, when I offered to meet with her husband, she told me it would not be necessary to talk to him. She said this in a way that let me know that, although the decision affected them both, it was hers primarily as it was her body, not his.

My secretary Jane has arrived precisely at nine o'clock. She wants to be called by her first name. She is present when I examine Mrs. Williams. Her reconstructed vagina still has sufficient depth and width for intercourse. Its lining has stayed smooth and is not painful to examine. The donor site on the buttocks from where I took the skin graft is in the bikini line and has healed well with only a faint scar. I am sorry to see Mrs. Williams leave this part of the country. I doubt that she and I will meet again, and I am also quite sure that she will not keep in touch even though I have asked her to. Not only was her condition uncommon, but so were her determination and courage. Perhaps because I have had a relatively comfortable life, I admire those who must overcome obstacles. I also think that someone seeing Mrs. Williams with her husband would never inquire about the reason for their not having children; the assumption would be that the husband, with his visible hand deformity, had prompted their decision. People are not always what they seem, a truism in plastic surgery.

Nevertheless, medicine, like other human activities, cannot be all highs. Not every incident in what transpires between a doctor and a patient would engross TV viewers. Yet, admittedly, much that the doctor considers routine would not seem so to a lay observer. These moments, relatively bland to the physician, are welcome, allowing us to resuscitate our inner selves.

My next patient today epitomizes the agreeable sequence in doctoring: an uncomplicated patient with an uncomplicated problem, simply solved. Mrs. Ruth Alpert came to me for an eyelidplasty, which she had four days ago. Her internist had referred her, as did some friends who had been my patients. She fits the usual category of those having this kind of surgery: she is white, fifty-five years old, and middle-class. Not many blacks or Orientals of that age come for facelifts or eyelidplasty. With regard to Orientals, this fact may be due to their aging better but not to their having lower incomes. In my town of Brookline, for example, there are many wealthy Chinese Americans, but those who have surgery to rejuvenate their faces are rare indeed. In fact, I have never done a facelift on someone who is Chinese. And, to my knowledge, they are not going en masse elsewhere in Boston for these procedures. Perhaps, in their culture, signs of aging, like age itself, command respect.

Now in her mid-fifties, Mrs. Ruth Alpert is stocky, her waist having triumphed over her will. Despite her graying hair, her round face makes her look several years younger. This is perhaps divine compensation for not having been born with high, prominent cheekbones that can give their possessor a startling beauty in early life but later carry their own liability of sagging, hollow cheeks, a condition that causes women to seek a plastic surgeon.

Mrs. Alpert is a lawyer, mother of two children in college, and the wife of a successful manufacturer, who came with her to the first consultation and is with her today. He is slightly shorter than his wife when she wears high heels, but his bushy white hair hides the difference. Their relationship seems good, easy and friendly. Each has a sense of humor. In general, those patients who come for elective surgery and lack even a trace of levity are apt to be the most demanding, difficult patients because they are likely demanding, difficult human beings. I try to avoid operating on them.

The Alperts spoke of the trips they have taken with their children in terms of a new experience the whole family shared, not in an attempt to let me know that they are sophisticated.

When Mrs. Alpert first met me, she joked about her being an attorney, "the kind that won't sue you." I bantered, "Don't disappoint me; all my patients file for malpractice. I rather expect it."

Malpractice suits are increasing distressingly. I have a colleague who refuses to operate electively on lawyers and their families. His decision is ostensibly to avoid malpractice, but it is really to retaliate against the legal profession because he was once sued successfully.

In my experience, attorneys are excellent patients. They are intelligent, cooperative, and you can always be sure that they have read the informed consent before signing. Perhaps I am wrong, but I think attorneys sue their own doctors disproportionately less frequently than other patients; perhaps they refrain to demonstrate magnanimity. At the risk of alienating my medical colleagues, I think that the presence of attorneys and the threat of malpractice have upgraded what our patients receive.

Here now is Mrs. Alpert, swollen and black and blue after her procedure, which was done under local anesthesia on an outpatient basis. She is presently sitting on the edge of the examining table and has discarded her dark glasses, the friend of the cosmetic patient. No matter how many operations the plastic surgeon may have performed, he or she will experience a twinge of anxiety at the first postoperative glance. Has anything gone wrong? Fortunately not. Mrs. Alpert has no pull down of the lower lids, no sign of infection or abnormal bleeding, no complaints about vision. Blindness after eyelidplasty is exceedingly rare, but I always warn patients about its possibility.

Mrs. Alpert tells me she has had "not too much pain," and then only the night of operation. I had prescribed Demerol, which she took for the first eighteen hours. She lies down, and I remove the stitches, never a pleasant experience for the patient. I recall a plastic surgeon in London with a very wealthy clientele who used to give them nitrous oxide at the time he took out their stitches, another example of how the rich often jeopardize their lives for comfort. I lay a cold, wet dressing on her eyes and ask whether she plans to return to work. "I'll do it at home for a while."

Most patients do not want others to know they have had aesthetic surgery. You can easily admit going to a dentist, and others will support you and perhaps admire your courage. Seeing a plastic surgeon, however, is like going to a psychiatrist. It may be the last thing you will tell your friends or they will reveal to you. Our society has its jokes about psychiatrists and plastic surgeons, but this indicates more anxiety than approval. The assumption is that the visit to the plastic surgeon is always for cosmetic surgery when, in fact, it may not be.

Our affluent culture provides the services to improve appearance but asks that they be paid for with guilt as well as money. Seeking a cosmetic operation is judged by many to be an act of vanity, and that, indeed, is the word that many patients use during their first consultation. The Puritan ethic, as we interpret it, would have us believe we should adapt to growing old or having an ugly feature as we must acquiesce to other acts of nature. We are too prone to demand of ourselves and others unreasonable toughness. Those with neurotic complaints, we think, should be able to "work it out." Although Mrs. Alpert is not racked by self-reproof for having had an eyelidplasty, she does not want to proclaim the fact to the world. For every patient having an aesthetic procedure, one of the major decisions is whether to tell and, if so, whom. Husbands whose wives have remained sexually faithful have been cuckolded over cosmesis. Even children may learn about it later or never. Patients have justified their keeping their act secret from their children by saying, "They do what they want; I'll do what I want." And it is true that parents are often more tolerant of their offspring's behavior than are their children of theirs when it is a question of this type of surgery.

Mrs. Alpert is the sort of patient who occupies an unremarkable place in a plastic surgeon's memory. She came for a specific purpose, an operation, which she has had successfully; she will be pleased afterward. Her history, our conversation and relationship have not elicited anything extraordinary. In a sense, she is not the right patient to include in a book. She is not spectacular; yet, for this reason alone, she merits attention, in order to chronicle the relief a plastic surgeon gets from a patient who remains forgettable. It is a sign of good surgery and smiling fate when a patient achieves a "routine" category. When I am with Mrs. Alpert, I would not want her to think she is a pedestrian event in my life. I work as hard as I can to be sure she thinks she is important to me, and she is for a while. But I also labor to be certain that her medical course is not worthy of reporting. I would willingly forgo the unpleasant excitement that comes with a complication. The media have distorted plastic surgery, robbed it of the commonplace, and made it overly thrilling. From Mrs. Alpert's viewpoint, the experience was not ordinary. Yet, if she wrote about it, it would probably be a sluggish tale of suburbia, perhaps told with a touch of humor but in a matter-of-fact way consistent with her personality and profession.

Nevertheless, I wonder also whether I have missed something with Mrs. Alpert. Does she have a momentous secret? An interdicted relationship? Does she gorge herself with chocolates or have an uncontrollable urge to smuggle ivory into this country? Sometimes on a rare day, when there have been a few cancellations and I have extra time, it is a small adventure to explore a patient like Mrs. Alpert.

A simple way of eliciting sometimes the most surprising information is to say to the most ordinary-looking individual, "I see from the record that you are a building inspector. Some people might think that your job is dull. Is it? What's the most unusual thing that ever happened to you in your work?" If the response is "I don't know," that usually ends the foray. Frequently, however, the reply can be decidedly out of the usual. Some patients are suspicious of a doctor who wants to know what the patient considers "too much," but others are grateful for the opportunity to release what they have bottled up for so long.

And some have never had many opportunities to be asked anything that could enhance their self-esteem. In their home and at work their lot has been to endure rather than to enjoy. The world seems to tell them, "Do your work, do not complain, get through life without causing a fuss." Perhaps they believe that they will be rewarded in heaven as they were not on earth.

In any relationship, and certainly that between patient and physician, each must decide how far to go. How much information does the physician require to do his or her job? But is only rendering a service such as an operation all that a patient wants, deserves, and should receive? While I do not like to pry, my expressing a concern that is not prurient about someone else's personal life does make that individual feel better and, I confess, does make my job more interesting. We all know how seldom during the course of a week another person is actually interested in what we do or feel. We may tell a friend to "have a good day," but our interest in the follow-up is meager. A visitor from England once observed: "In my country, we are very reserved, and we believe everyone should have his own privacy. In your country, you are very friendly, but you probably don't really care any more than we do about the next person."

I do care about people, but I admit that on occasion I enter an inner arena where I probably should not be. While I cannot justify this intrusion, it does result from an enjoyment of people and a desire to know them more than superficially. I aim for that self, at the center of the circle, not the fifth concentric self. Yet I do not feel that, in return for my services, a patient must offer his or her soul for my inspection and gratification.

chapter 4

Once, while discussing this kind of book with an editor, I had difficulty in convincing him that not every patient is a penitent, seeking salvation, physically or emotionally, through an anatomic change. Dr. Norman Bernstein, a friend and psychiatrist at Northwestern, made the point in a chapter for a book I edited on long-term results in plastic surgery that rhinoplasty, for example, could be pivotal in a patient's life or it could also be unimportant depending upon the internal and external events at that particular time for that individual. What would happen, for example, if a patient's father, who opposed a rhinoplasty, dropped dead a week after it had been done? A macabre thought, but in that situation, the patient would most likely curse even the best technical result. Decidedly, the patient's nose job, to use the loathsome vernacular, would not be a forgotten episode.

When Maxwell Maltz, a prominent plastic surgeon in

the 1920s and also the founder of psychocybernetics, wrote his autobiography, *Doctor Pygmalion,* he described the kind of plastic surgeon who no longer exists—if, indeed, he ever did. That altering an unattractive feature can lead to other important changes in a person's life, I do not contest. Nevertheless, the idea that the miraculous and brilliant plastic surgeon, a veritable sculptor of the flesh, can transmute the mundane human into the magnificent is farfetched. Not even a romantic like me can pretend otherwise. Many patients, it is true, do seek miracles. They may incite a vulnerable and egotistical plastic surgeon to believe himself or herself a deity capable of delivering marvels. Yet most plastic surgeons I know are not that foolish. They work hard and carefully, as do many others in various occupations. They are professionals, and like any professional, they perform well most of the time.

Offsetting those few patients who think of the plastic surgeon as a deity are those many who consider him merely a provider of services, like an accountant, an interior decorator, or an auto body mechanic. Although most plastic surgeons do not think of themselves either as celestial beings or tradespeople, they nevertheless wish to be important in their patient's life, and they are, for the moment—just as the pilot who is in charge of your plane may be the focus of your thoughts while you are in flight. A doctor should remember that he or she can do an intimate physical examination of a patient and not be an intimate of the patient. By that, I mean that if a gynecologist does an internal examination or a general surgeon performs sigmoidoscopy the patient does not necessarily consider the physician either a confidant or a friend. I do not deplore the fact that there is a difference between a doctor's being friendly and being a friend. That there are boundaries and barriers is a safeguard for the patient and the physician.

While Mrs. Alpert's eyelidplasty might have not been wild enough for a Hollywood picture, it does have an astonishing aspect. That is the matter of trust. Patients who do not know me personally until their consultation will soon place themselves under my care. In a world that knows too much of betrayal, this evidence of faith is more than refreshing. It is not I alone who am responsible for this phenomenon, but generations of physicians who have not misled or abused their patients.

Until just a few decades ago, patients in our country had little choice about their doctor, whom they saw only in crisis. The great increase in the number of physicians as well as the emphasis now on preventive medicine and visiting one's doctor sooner and more regularly have made medicine elective for more patients and physicians.

I remember one consultation for an elective operation of a relatively minor nature from my first year in practice.

Miss Dabney had a small lesion on her left forearm. Her answers to my questions were as precise as one might expect from a librarian, which she was, at a nearby college. A stocky, plain woman in her late fifties, she had an energetic masculine quality. Her hair was closely cropped and gray-black, her hands large, her legs like pikes encased in heavy brown stockings, her feet encased in shoes with tips that matched the square-cut of her tweed suit. It was not surprising that she rode a bike to work and devoted her weekends to bird-watching. The Lord, if you are a believer, had installed in her the best of systems, all functioning in top order. I doubted that she ever had menstrual cramps, but I did not inquire because it was irrelevant. I wondered why this tiny growth on her arm, which even to most lay people would look totally benign, had brought her to see me. I did not have to wait long for an explanation.

"Miss Davis, who shares my house, had a mother who died of melanoma. Edna thinks that this little thing on my arm has grown, and she made me call you. You operated on a friend of hers. If it hadn't been for Edna, I wouldn't be here."

She also said that this was the first time she had been to a doctor since she was a child. I told her that her ordinary-looking mole was nothing to worry about, but I did think that it should be removed since someone had noticed that it had increased in size. I then arranged for the procedure, a week later. I thought that would be all there was to it, but she telephoned the next day and insisted on speaking to me.

"Doctor, I am sorry that I cannot let you operate on me because I enjoyed our visit and respect your ability. But I looked up your birth date in the *Directory of Medical Specialists,* which I have in the library. It is unfortunate, but we do not match from the astrological point of view." She told me that I was a Virgo. So great was my astonishment that I forgot what she was.

"I do hope you understand," she said.

I managed an automatic "Of course." Even though I realized that her not having me operate on me was due to factors beyond my control, I did feel uncomfortable and remembered those prep school dances when the girl I wanted to dance with already had her card filled.

As I now look down at my desk, I see a message my

secretary left for me. Mrs. Beatrice Wittry once again changed her appointment for an eyelidplasty. Since this is the third time she has done this, I shall tell my secretary not to reschedule her, ever. I believe she is in conflict about the procedure, and I will call her later to tell her not to push herself into an elective operation. I usually advise patients that, if they are fifty-fifty, or even seventy-thirty in favor of having an operation, they should not have it. A 10 percent or perhaps 20 percent margin of doubt is understandable. Patients with significant misgivings may do well postoperatively if the operation and the result approach their expectations, but should there be a complication, they may accuse the doctor of having talked them into it, and they may be right. Fortunately, I have enough patients who are enthusiastic, or relatively so, about the prospect of an operation that I do not need to depend upon those who are unsure.

Some plastic surgeons refuse to return a patient's money if she or he cancels the procedure without sufficient notice. While that may be financially advantageous to the surgeon, it also may ensure him of operating on a patient who really should get away. I do not charge patients if they cancel a procedure, although I do bill them for their initial consultation. It seems wrong to exact a payment for a service not rendered. It also does little to enhance one's reputation.

My experience with the next patient, Miss Ida Gelkin, has done little to enhance either my reputation or satisfaction.

She is a remarkable eighty-five-year-old, with a heavy Yiddish accent, who enters with her usual determined gait. Although she has always been small, the years have diminished her even more. Yet she remains compact and forceful, like a former gymnast, which she never was.

Miss Gelkin's mother had witnessed the pogroms around Kiev, and Miss Gelkin and her sister immigrated here when they were children. They later worked in factories, never married, and lived together. Miss Gelkin has frequently said, "I have always been a hard worker. I have never had it easy, doctor." She is immaculate and dresses in a fastidious 1945 style. Seeing her reminds me of what one elderly patient said to me: "I am careful how I dress. But who looks?" We know that we are old when people react to us like a neuter object. To be young is to have one's sexuality taken seriously. Emerson noted, "We do not count a man's years until he has nothing else to count."

Ida Gelkin is a connoisseur of doctors even though, until recently, she has been basically healthy. She pays homage to every complaint, even minor, for which she seeks the opinions of at least two physicians. She keeps in condition, I think, simply by going for medical appointments.

She was referred to me a few years ago for a basal cell carcinoma of her face. I excised it, and she was happy that after a year the scar was not noticeable.

She returned a few months ago with two similar lesions, one on each shin. Her legs were edematous because she also had congestive heart failure. With proper treatment from her internist, her circulation improved. Her skin cancers, however, were large but presumably could be cured either by irradiation or surgery. The operation would have involved a skin graft for closure, but Miss Gelkin refused. She had irradiation, which made the basal cell cancer disappear, but two years afterward she noted redness and itching in the area of treatment. Because of the possibility of recurrent cancer, she underwent a small biopsy, and the skin subsequently broke down so that an ulcer formed. This is a difficult problem because, as a result of the previous X-ray therapy, wound-healing is abnormal. The local blood supply is poor, and the tissues either fail to heal or close slowly, especially in a patient of Miss Gelkin's age. A skin graft, which ordinarily would be successful, will not take over an irradiated ulcer where the vascularity is meager. Miss Gelkin needs the rotation of a muscle into the ulcer bed, but this will require hospitalization.

Understandably, she is upset, and predictably she would like the opinion of another physician. In fact, I give her the names of two other plastic surgeons to whom I am happy to refer her. Today I change her dressing. There has been very little healing over these past few weeks. I explain once again to Miss Gelkin about the problem of wound-healing and about the necessity for a flap of tissue to obtain wound coverage. For Miss Gelkin, several explanations are nevertheless insufficient. However, after we make arrangements for her to see one of the surgeons whom I have recommended, she appears satisfied.

As she leaves, she does not disappoint me. She always turns the wrong way, and I always redirect her. This is her idiosyncrasy, a minor one, well within the predictable range of behavior for a patient. She has not, for example, cursed me or flung an ashtray at my head. Patients and their doctors relate to each other in ways that are expected. When they do not, it is a good reason for them to separate, if they have ever joined.

Miss Gelkin makes me somewhat uncomfortable not just because I have referred her elsewhere but because I consider her somewhat comical. I feel guilty at being amused, not by her plight, but by her mannerisms. Does this reflect the fact that my emotional commitment to her is superficial?

That Miss Gelkin will be seeing another doctor characterizes the practice of medicine and surgery today. All patients, not just plastic surgical, want to be better informed than those a decade ago. Frequently more than one physician participates in their enlightenment. A doctor who becomes offended at a patient's seeking another opinion is behaving anachronistically. Patients for elective plastic surgery may go to a few doctors in order to get someone they like, perhaps at the price they want, for the result they expect, by the method they prefer. In my experience, a major stimulus for another opinion is to obtain a desired outcome.

The drawback is that the patient develops a shopper's mentality and regards the aesthetic operation as a commodity. The process of wandering through the mall of medicine will lead the patient to think of the operation in the same terms as an item in a store. The person is foolish to believe that he or she is purchasing a stove. The final result of a surgical procedure depends on many factors that are beyond anyone's control. The surgeon, at best, cannot regulate or even guide wound-healing. Furthermore, if a customer does not like a stove or it does not work, usually there is a guarantee and it can be returned and replaced with something the same or even better. Not so the outcome of the aesthetic operation, which, if it fails, can make the patient look worse. And this, for someone who wanted to look better, is a genuine catastrophe.

The person journeying from one doctor to another while attempting to decide on having a facelift, for example, may ultimately locate a surgeon who will satisfy that quest for certainty. That doctor may give the patient assurances beyond the dictates of reality. With enough persistence and sufficient money, any patient, except the most bizarre, will find a compliant surgeon. Some are flattered that a patient has come to them after having been seen by other surgeons, especially those with known reputations. That patient is vulnerable to an insecure or conniving surgeon, who puffs up himself or herself by undertaking this "discriminating," yet demanding, patient. He or she becomes less of a patient than a consumer, who may have purchased a three-legged horse.

Patients for cosmetic surgery have another peculiar characteristic: they are usually in good health, which they willingly risk in order to improve their self-image. The plastic surgeon thereby deviates from most of his surgical colleagues, who traditionally operate only when the patient is unwell. Operating on the healthy is paradoxically what makes the surgery of appearance a dangerous enterprise. Patients expect all to go well, even after you have told them what can go wrong, even after they have signed an informed consent that lists in ferocious detail the complications of a specific procedure.

But it is also true that every surgeon doing cosmetic surgery expects success or he would not undertake a procedure that could end poorly. Because his patients are reluctant or ashamed to have an operation when they are not truly sick, they frequently express their fear of possible divine retribution. A few may openly say, "I hope all goes well and God doesn't punish me." Other patients are more subtle: "Doctor, after the facelift, will I suddenly wake up one morning and look worse than I ever did if I never had the operation at all?" In their fantasies, they have had to atone for tampering with what they presume nature and God ordained.

This dilemma between what is mutable and immutable causes the individual patient anguish and divides the larger society. How much time and how many resources should we spend for bread or chocolate? Even a so-called subsistent, primitive culture, battling daily to survive, still plays. In fact, for emotional and physical renewal, that type of lean culture needs diversion.

To my knowledge, no society has ignored the body; none has accepted it and left it alone. Universally, there are proscriptions concerning dress and physical changes. A village elder will rub carbon into a fresh wound for a tribal marking. My operation on Mrs. Alpert's eyes, though done in an elaborate facility and with the ultimate in aseptic technique and modern technology, is nevertheless a social convention, at least for a certain group of people in our heterogenous culture. Scarification confers a group identity; so does looking young or less old. The tribal surgeon, however, has the satisfaction of knowing that the visible effects of his procedure will last as long as his patient lives; not so I, for much of my work. Time and gravity are inexorable. The skin will stretch, and alas, gone will be my surgical accomplishment.

All this reminds me that, even though I seem isolated in my office, I am here performing social acts. Whatever individual flair I have, I function within a prescribed context. This is true also for the patient.

I was supposed to see Michael Gold at nine o'clock, but

he is not here and probably will not come. Most busy practitioners consider it a welcome hiatus when a patient does not show up, but in my work, I am concerned that the person might be dissatisfied. Such, however, is not the case with Michael. I treated him more than fifteen years ago, and he had a good result. I really was not sure why he was returning to see me today.

I remember our first encounter and especially his last appointment. Six months before then, while he was coming home at night from the college library, two predators held him up. He resisted, but a knife slashed his hand and severed two extensor tendons. When the police brought him to the emergency ward, he was frightened of a possible operation. He was also angry: "If I had another chance, I would kill the bastards who did this." I tried to call his parents in the Bronx, but Michael predicted that they would not be home. "They never are." From what he had told me, I assumed that his father, an insurance salesman, and his mother, an executive secretary, lived separately at the same address. Michael learned to be independent and cynical as well.

In the emergency ward, he said to me, "I am sorry that I am keeping you up late, doc, but that's how you pay your bills."

He was more correct than he had imagined, since I had been in practice only a couple of years.

Neither Michael's postoperative course nor his operation was unusual. After wearing a splint for five weeks, he quickly regained full use of his hand.

He was not the easiest person to talk to, because he tried to control conversation, not so much to dominate but to avoid personal questions. He told me that he was studying business administration and that he would like to have a job where "you don't have to deal daily with people and their crap." When he said this, he looked at me.

On his last visit a few weeks before he was to graduate, I asked whether he knew what he would be doing—not a popular question with those under twenty-five.

"I really don't know, but I'm sure I'll find something that I like. Let me ask you this, doc, what does all that you're doing get you? What does it all mean for you? You know, being the big doctor, the right connections, the office—all the fixings—but where will it get you? Where are you heading?"

What he said did not surprise me as much as that he said it. With some reluctance, I had asked myself the same questions. To maintain our balance while treading the earth for the few decades most of us have, we usually avoid such intense self-inquiry.

"I agree with you, Mike, that all this is ephemeral, but since we are here and since time will demolish each of us, I would rather be doing what I am doing than most other things." My response to his remarks made me think of what my English teacher at prep school had told our class. He said that his family doctor once compared his life and its impermanence to placing a finger in a glass of water and then withdrawing it, with no trace remaining.

Michael did not let me linger in the past.

"You are kidding yourself, doc. Fifty years from now you won't be here and maybe I won't, and what difference does it make?"

I gave him the obvious response. "That night that you came in, Mike, if I had that attitude, I'm not sure what type of operation you would have received."

Since he did not refute that argument, I technically won, although I had not really answered his existential questions.

Now, twenty years later, I am at the same stand. I wonder what Michael is doing, and I am sorry that he did not keep his appointment because I wanted to find out.

Unlike general practitioners, I do not have many patients who come back just to say hello. As I mentioned before, the relationship of a plastic surgeon to the patient may be intense, but it is usually brief unless the patient has had many operations over a great number of years. Performing a yearly checkup and treating all members of a family are not characteristic of my specialty. Yet pleasant surprises do occur. When I was a resident at the Brigham, I had as a patient a sixteen-year-old-boy who had severely injured his wrist while trying to rob a warehouse. He was a model juvenile delinquent. What was especially memorable about him was his extensive four-letter-word vocabulary.

The celestial computer had arranged for a middle-aged nurse to take care of him. This particular nurse was, in actuality, a nun who had returned to the hospital to modernize her skills. Because the patient, Bill Marlow, had refused all suggestions as well as medications, the other nurses thought that he would be an admirable case for Sister Louise. In her first dealings with him, she became the target of his verbal assault. Immediately, she did what her mother must have done to her brothers: she grabbed him by the neck, led him to the sink, and washed his mouth out with soap. "You will never speak to me or anybody else like that again."

This forcible ablution engendered a miracle. Bill became cooperative, and even though he never attained the status of a Cicero, he shed many of his favorite epithets. He became dependent on Sister Louise, who went with him to physical therapy and watched his progress with a hawklike diligence even after he had left the hospital.

I lost touch with Sister Louise and Bill until seventeen years later when he walked into my office with his thirteen-year-old daughter, who had a "mole" on her cheek. He was now happily married and the manager of a firm that sold adding machines. He said, "I guess I was some kind of a hell-raiser when you first met me. If it hadn't been for people like you and Sister Louise, I never would have made it in life." I realized that he had included me only to be polite. Today, if Sister Louise were alive to wash other patients' mouths, she and the hospital would be sued for physical abuse. Yet by her actions, she had demonstrated to Bill a profound commitment to his welfare, something he had never experienced.

Bill had had no expectations. Many patients do expect reasonable care and results and still others have extraordinary expectations.

About fifteen years ago, a man from South America consulted me about a problem that he described to my secretary as "very personal." When I met him, it was obvious that he came from the moneyed stratum. Though small, he dressed in high style, with manners consistent with his affluence and gentility. He entered my office and left it within six minutes.

"I have come to see you about something that has been bothering me for some time. I hope you will be able to help me."

"What is it?"

"Doctor, it will seem strange to you, but I looked up my family history and I found that way back we have black blood in it."

"Oh," I murmured.

"My question is, can you change my skin? Can you give me the skin from a completely white man?"

"No," I said.

"Thank you," he replied, stood up, shook my hand, and told my secretary to bill him at his home address.

His expectations were unrealistic, but he is not alone. Many who frequent plastic surgeons are sure that we can do the impossible. Anything is possible in a society that can place a man on the moon and can waft a spray to get rid of body odors.

A few years ago, Eileen Tracy, a pert twenty-two-year-old bartender, asked me on a Wednesday if I could operate on her that evening to do an augmentation mammoplasty because in two days she had to fly to Florida to get married. She told me that, unlike some of her friends, she and her future husband had never been sexually intimate. She used "falsies" and wanted to avoid the chagrin on the night of reckoning. I told her it would be impossible to schedule an operation like that so quickly and to have her recover sufficiently for a marriage and a honeymoon, which they had planned. She did not want to disappoint her future husband, who was a jockey—an occupation that prompts fantasies of the conjugal night.

That consultation with Eileen Tracy makes me think of Cindy Walsh, also a young woman of Irish descent. However, Cindy, who was twenty-five, had been married and divorced. She also wanted an augmentation mammoplasty.

Her story was singularly tragic. She had married Terry, whom she had known since high school. Both families were delighted with the match, and the wedding was joyful.

As they were returning from their honeymoon in Florida, another car struck them on the driver's side, and they turned over. Cindy broke her leg, but Terry fractured his lower back and became paraplegic. For eight years, Cindy said, "I did the right thing. I am a Catholic, and so is he. But I couldn't take it anymore. He became abusive, and I think it was his way of setting me free. He began to drink, and he wouldn't go to a psychiatrist. I was willing to have sex with him, but he said he 'wouldn't inflict' himself on me because he felt like a 'cripple.' "

Finally, she went to a priest who told her that he did not have the right to participate in a dissolution of a marriage but that there was a higher law than even the Church. "God understands more than we do on earth," he said.

Though divorced, she sees Terry every week, and he has been less self-destructive. Her augmentation mammoplasty, which I did later, was part of her rebirth. Getting a new body was symbolic to her of the good that she hoped would come in her new life.

With every patient who asks me to modify his or her body, I assess timing and expectations. Why does he or she want this operation now? What result does he or she anticipate, not just intellectually but emotionally?

Some patients are obvious ones to avoid operating on. Such a person is Mr. Radford, concerning whom Jane has left a note on my desk: "Please see Mr. Radford's letter," which is clipped to a bill from our office.

I received your statement for the consultation, and it is outrageous. You charged me $50, when you did nothing for me and I do not intend to pay, and if you wish to pursue this further, please do so through my attorney [name and address given].

Sincerely yours,
R. M. RADFORD

The amenity of "Sincerely yours" is absurd in its hypocrisy. His note should say, "Yours with intent to murder." Such a letter, especially when I was first in practice, used to anger me. It also meant a loss of income. In those youthful days I would interpret such a letter as a personal insult and a violation of the basic principles of barter: paying for what one receives. Mr. Radford obviously felt he had not received anything from the consultation. While I am not happy with such behavior, I am more sanguine now. In comparison with many other human follies, Mr. Radford's act is a mild aberration.

I couldn't forget Mr. Radford, a minister in his mid-forties, with an unpleasantly forceful voice. To emphasize his words, he would nod his head in a vigorous staccato. Though of average build, he filled the room. He told me he had been recently divorced and had moved to Boston several months before. From his referring physician, I learned the cause of his departure was an affair that became big news in his small town. The reverend wore a toupé and wanted hair transplants, a rhinoplasty, a facelift, an eyelidplasty, a chin implant, and revision of old scars from an auto accident. In short, he wanted rebirth in a single session of multiple operations. I tried to make him understand that to do all this at one time would be inadvisable. As gently as I could, I offered the observation that many things seemed to be happening in his life and that he appeared "unrelaxed." I frankly thought that he was in a manic phase and might soon be going through a depression. In addition, he had said that in the past few weeks he had been bothered by insomnia, which can be a clue to this kind of illness. I suggested that he see a psychiatrist.

He responded in a fury. "I am not crazy. You are, if you think that I am. Are you or are you not a plastic surgeon? What is so unusual about what I am asking for you to do?"

I explained that each of these requests was not unusual by itself, but his presenting a long list, along with so many other recent changes in his life, might indicate that "perhaps your emotions are in flux." He stomped out of the office, but his final humility was having to return for the umbrella that he had forgotten. This might have been an unconscious equivalent of having the operation.

Today I will tell my secretary not to bill him further. My decision is not so much based on the fact that I would have to resort to legal means as on the fact that the amount is relatively small compared to the effort required to collect it.

While my experience with the reverend might have a dash of comedy, there is more than a touch of tragedy. He wanted to solve all his problems by changing his appearance. His expectations were unreal and his insight lacking. My interaction with him also illustrates the difficulty of refusing to operate on some patients and the even greater ordeal of successfully referring them to a psychiatrist. Sometimes patients accept seeing a psychologist or a social worker more easily. The word "psychiatrist" connotes for them serious mental illness. A recommendation to see a psychiatrist, no matter how it is phrased, is not pleasant to receive. Frequently, if I know the referring physician, I enlist his or her help. Even then, the task is not easy.

Unlike those who are contemplating operations in other fields of surgery, those who come for a cosmetic procedure will use a second opinion in order to obtain an operation, not to prevent an unnecessary one. According to the definition of "medically necessary," every aesthetic operation is medically unnecessary. Insurance companies, for example, do not care whether it is "necessary" to maintain emotional health; in their rule book, that does not warrant their paying for the operation. If a seventeen-year-old had an enormous, ugly nose that partly accounted for her depression, there would still be no third-party payment; yet the services of a psychiatrist would be covered for the first $500, according to the Blue Shield code in Massachusetts. Inanities and inconsistencies are rife in these matters, but this is also so in most areas of human activity.

I cannot help musing that the reverend's note to me may contain an unintended, unwelcome message about the direction my life has taken when I glance at the picture of Albert Schweitzer on my desk. At the completion of my general surgical residency, before starting my plastic surgical training in Pittsburgh, I spent a couple of months with Dr. Schweitzer in Lambaréné as his surgeon. What had prompted me to apply there, years before I actually went, was the frustration of being an intern: the uncomfortable combination of too many tasks, too little time for contemplation, and the reality of being one of many in a university hospital with an embarrassingly high ratio of doctors to patients. Three years later, when I heard that Dr. Schweitzer actually needed a surgeon and when others more senior than I could not go, I eagerly volunteered. I am sure my ability to converse in French helped to secure the position when Erica Anderson, Dr. Schweitzer's long-time friend, biographer, and photographer, came to interview me.

The plan was for me to leave in three weeks. Dr. Schweitzer had invited my wife, and although we did not yet have children, she chose not to go because she was a social worker and had committed herself to the hospital, which could not hire a replacement in such a short time. It did not seem right for her to abandon her duty in order to travel to see Dr. Schweitzer, whose name was synonymous with duty. However, to be honest, we both now regret her not having accompanied me. The condition that I had to meet at the Brigham, where I was a resident, was to find someone to cover for me. Fortunately, another senior resident was voracious for more surgical experience, and he was overjoyed to take my place.

Dr. Schweitzer's reasons for going to Africa were considerably different from mine, which included a longing to meet the great jungle healer, a need for adventure, as well as a wish to be helpful. In his autobiography and in his conversations with me, he reiterated that what prompted him to go to Africa was not only his desire to help the blacks, whom he considered the quintessential sufferers, but also his discomfort in finding self-fulfillment in the usual philanthropic work of an overdeveloped society. I could identify somewhat with that sentiment. Schweitzer needed something more than church bazaars. Yet he realized that not everyone should make working with the disadvantaged in Africa or a similar place his or her goal. In his words, "From those to whom more is given, more is expected," and he based this expression on Christ's example.

My two months with Dr. Schweitzer was more than adequate compensation for all the arduous years of pre-medicine, medical school, and postgraduate training. Although Harvard has many genuine heroes, it has also many more whose status is greater than their stature, those who have mastered the system, power brokers without intrinsic greatness or humaneness, qualities that, as far as I am concerned, Dr. Schweitzer had in abundance. Others, if robbed of their props, would collapse. Not so Dr. Schweitzer, whose peculiar misfortune was to have lived long enough to be faulted for his paternalistic attitudes toward blacks, for his failure to train enough of them as professionals, and for his reluctance to modernize his hospital. While these are valid criticisms, they should not overshadow his contributions of more than fifty years in the jungle, especially when one realizes that those who reproach him have usually done little more than send a check to the NAACP.

Dr. Schweitzer never claimed to be the ultimate Christian; he admitted his deficiencies but also exercised his right to fulfill himself in his own way. He had the correct type of self-fulfillment. Too many of us have the wrong kind, which excludes everybody but ourselves.

Despite the ennobling experience of being at Lambaréné with Dr. Schweitzer, I concluded that I could not emulate his life. I was already a hooked bourgeois, dependent upon material things that to me were necessities, though for most of the world they were luxuries. I also wanted to remain close to my parents and to be able to educate future children without having to send them away. My wife shared these feelings. I would be dishonest if I did not admit that my evaluation of my strengths, weaknesses, and needs displeased me then and displeases me now. There are too many base metals in me. Yet no alchemist, and certainly not I, could change my ingredients by that time in my life, even though I might have modified their proportion.

Eventually most doctors gravitate toward what gives them the most gratification; there are various satisfactions for various people and for the same person at different times. In my specialty, some find the most self-realization doing facelifts, eyelidplasties, rhinoplasties, and breast augmentations, receiving a few thousand dollars for each procedure; for others, professional and personal satisfaction comes from performing only hand surgery; for still others—most plastic surgeons like myself—happiness is a combination of cosmetic and reconstructive work. Yet it would be a rare plastic surgeon who would not want the income that aesthetic surgery readily gives.

The challenge is not just to build an aesthetic practice but to enjoy the image that comes with it. If one truly believes that temporarily rejuvenating a sagging face is rehabilitation, then one feels pride, not guilt, about his or her work. If one feels some shame in earning so much money from cosmetic operations, one can donate earnings and time to charity, as expiation. Some colleagues have told me that periodically volunteering as a surgeon in an undeveloped country was their way of handling the conflict.

Everyone eventually makes some sort of an accommodation, even if it is not perfect.

Those who perform mostly reconstructive procedures usually do not need to justify their professional labors to themselves or to others. But they frequently have to deal with their resentment of their "cosmetic" colleagues who make more money. One surgeon known for reconstruction believes himself the epitome of the Christian physician. He has honored every Commandment but the last; his covetousness consumes him.

My generation of plastic surgeons expected to perform the entire spectrum of reconstruction and cosmesis. Our field was not so fragmented as it is today. With time, however, we found that we were doing more aesthetic operations and fewer reconstructive. This phenomenon fits a basic law of medical practice: the younger the doctor, the more emergency cases he gets; the older the doctor, the more elective cases. But plastic surgery still permits exceptions to the rule and some picking and choosing. I know, for example, a younger plastic surgeon who has determined how many procedures of what type to do in order to earn the most while at the same time projecting a satisfactory image to himself and others. Without being innovative, he does mostly rhinoplasties and excisions of skin lesions. But he, in addition to his patients, has paid a price. He has become professionally old before his time. Nevertheless, he has avoided what is now the plight of many in Massachusetts—being paid disproportionately little for emergency and reconstructive work, in contrast to what one can earn from elective cosmetic operations.

Whatever pattern of practice a plastic surgeon or any physician chooses necessarily eliminates other alternatives. One cannot go down both branches of a two-forked road at the same time. I keep Schweitzer's picture on my desk to remind me of the larger vision I should have of myself, my work, and the world. At the same time, it is an unwelcome cue to my unhappy thoughts about the pettiness and even insignificance of some of my labors and much of my life. I have enough insight to recognize the conflict, but not enough wisdom or courage to resolve it.

chapter 5

My secretary rings to remind me that I have a full morning of patients and that, unless I hasten, I will be late for the operating room. Fortunately, my next patient, Melissa Pearson, who comes because of a skin lesion, should not take much of my time and will probably not need much of my emotional support. Short and unimposing, with large glasses, Melissa is in the first year of college and is the daughter of a physician, who was concerned about a mole growing on Melissa's waist and the repeated irritation caused by her belt. With her is her boyfriend, to whom she turns for support and guidance. That he is a pre-medical student elevates his status in her eyes. She is reticent, lets me do the talking, and probably is passive with important males in her life. Her father, whom I know, is very dominating.

Melissa's lesion looks benign and will be easy to remove on an outpatient basis under local anesthesia, but she will have a scar. The problem with these small growths, even though they are not serious, is that the patient expects a plastic surgeon to excise them without leaving a trace. In this particular instance, however, Melissa has heard from her father about scarring and is prepared for this event. Some patients are not.

She tells me she is frightened that she might have cancer and is quickly relieved to know that she does not. Since her problem is relatively minor, I spend little time with her, as I had expected. I have barely entered her life. We have not strayed from the small matter at hand. Our mutual expectations as patient and physician, as well as the nature of her problem, have kept her consultation circumscribed.

She telephoned my office about a growth; the secretary scheduled her for a fifteen-minute visit, and I have conformed to the expected pattern of my day. Melissa is a transitory patient, unless something goes wrong in her care. Some physicians might find this experience frustrating because they feel they are a physician only when they become immersed in a patient with a major illness. For me, one of the advantages of plastic surgery is to be able to see more than a single patient in the course of an hour rather than just one, as psychiatrists and cardiologists do.

Melissa does not desperately need me, in contrast to my next patient, Miss Clara Svenrud, who once did. My secretary announces her; Clara is, in fact, a secretary herself. She and I have become medical intimates over the years. She had the misfortune of receiving irradiation for acne when she was seventeen. She was a victim of her times, as most of us are. We may benefit from what is current, or it can take away our lives. Some may die in a war, others from leukemia because their town failed to remove toxic waste. When Clara was young, irradiation was an accepted treatment for acne. In fact, her family took her from Massachusetts to New York City, to obtain the best X-ray therapy, although none would have been the best—a realization that came decades later.

Miss Svenrud developed extensive radiation-induced cancers of the skin of the midportion of her face, leading to surgical removal of her entire nose. In those days, we did not have the ability to take tissue from one location and to revascularize it by immediately joining its artery and vein to those at another site. She underwent the truly classic operation of having nasal reconstruction by means of tissue attached from her arm. She had to remain with her head turned to her left shoulder for about two and a half weeks until the flap of arm tissue obtained its new blood supply from the face. This operation was described by Tagliacozzi in 1497. He was a great pioneer in our specialty, and his book on nasal reconstruction was really the first textbook in our field. Because he was a professor of surgery at the University of Bologna, he gave our specialty the beginnings of an academic status. We are still trying to secure it.

Tagliacozzi was not the first to rebuild the nose; it had been done from the arm even a few centuries before the fifteenth and still earlier from the forehead or cheek, a method described in the Indian literature, the Susurta, about 600 B.C. In Miss Svenrud's case, it would not have been a good idea to use the forehead or cheek for the needed tissue, because those areas also had irradiation and might later have spawned carcinomas.

It is understandable that before going through the cumbersome procedure of nasal reconstruction Miss Svenrud gave it much thought. She would not only have to endure the first operation, remaining with her face attached to her upper arm, but would also require another operation to detach the flap, and still another to fold it on itself in order to fashion the nostrils. Although these last two procedures are relatively minor and could be done under local anesthesia, they nevertheless are operations to the patient. What decided Clara to proceed with nasal rebuilding and to discard forever her nasal prosthesis was an unpleasant incident. One day while she was on the subway, a small boy asked his mother, "How come the light shines through that lady's nose?" I pity not only the patient for having heard it but the mother for having to deal with it.

I have done about a dozen of these forehead flaps to rebuild the nose; doubtless, Tagliacozzi did more. Miss Svenrud had the benefit of anesthesia and of modern aseptic techniques, but because the head and neck are richly supplied with blood, the chance for infection is low; this fact allowed Tagliacozzi to be successful. Nevertheless, in those days, the pain must have been a major consideration. Ether made its debut only 135 years ago.

For the past decade, Miss Svenrud and I have communicated not just about medical matters. She sends me letters from time to time to let me know how she is doing, not just with respect to her nose. I get an occasional card when she takes a trip, especially to Paris, a city for which she knows I have a special fondness.

For Clara, the tragedy was having to witness the progressive loss of her face and learning to deal with social rejection and isolation. She has had the benefit of warm family life. She had been a popular teenager, and even today she is extremely attractive except for the nose, which, I must admit, although it might be fairly good for a reconstruction, is still not an ideal organ. I can remember that, when I was examining her for places to take a skin graft to use in conjunction with rebuilding the nose, I had noted that she was beautifully proportioned. How else can I express it without using a cliché or seeming lecherous? During working hours we physicians are allowed to speak and think of integument but not of flesh. I console myself with the military maxim that any wall can be breached. I cannot defend against all thoughts.

Clara once told me she had met a married man at work for whom she had an obvious liking. "Of course, no one suspects us," she had said. These words indicated to me not just that they were careful about their meetings but that her self-esteem was so poor, because of her nose, that she believed no one would ever seriously think any man would want her. She lives with her aged but devoted parents, and I wonder what she will do about her loneliness after they die. She seems less creative about arrangements for love than are some of my patients. At this time, she appears content to wait for the foraging male. Whatever the circumstances, she will probably hesitate in conflict and perhaps capitulate in astonishment.

While I have these personal thoughts about her, I am careful not to let her know them. Professionalism above all else!

The purpose of her visit is to be sure no cancers have recurred. Fortunately, they have not. Outwardly she has adjusted to her man-made nose. She seems pleased with her present job and mentions nothing about her social life. This afternoon she will permit herself a minor fling—

some shopping in the city. She comes from a small town in Massachusetts.

Our interaction today has lost the early intensity it had when I was more important in her life, when I removed the cancer and reconstructed her nose. This is as it should be since she is rehabilitated and presumably well. Yet I admit that I miss the keenness that comes only as the battle takes place. The bonding is then the strongest. Now, for both of us, there is more affection but less passionate commitment. She is satisfied without more surgery, and I do not see the need for any. We both have made the break.

Another patient, another life adventure, takes Clara's place—Jamie and her mother, Mrs. Jacqueline Hebert. I have not seen Jamie since I operated on her cleft lip when she was three months old, now ten years ago. The family has moved away, but Mr. Hebert had to return to Boston on business and they arranged this appointment. Jamie is a charming girl with an easy smile, long auburn hair, and active, large eyes. She already has her mother's looks and mannerisms that will magnetize men. Although Jamie is ostensibly pleased with her appearance, she would benefit from another procedure to improve the scar on her lip and to elevate the slope of her left nostril. Nevertheless, Jamie wants no operation now, and her mother tells me obliquely that she has many friends at school and socially her repaired cleft presents no problems at this time.

She is the only child, and there was no family history of clefting. Her parents consulted a geneticist who encouraged them to have more children, but the Heberts decided that Jamie was enough.

I am especially careful in what I say to Jamie. It is important not to emphasize imperfections, especially since she does not seem aware of them and certainly does not want an operation. Mrs. Hebert and I agree that we will keep this visit only a visit and not a prelude to surgery. I offer to regroup with the Heberts later if they wish. Jamie's mother understands that I have in mind possible unpleasantness when Jamie begins dating.

Some patients need to maintain the tie. They even send pictures of themselves or their family.

This morning's mail contains a handwritten letter and a photo of a small baby. It is from Betsy MacGinnis, whom I knew by her maiden name when I did a breast reduction on her. The gist of the letter is that she and her husband, whom I have never met, now live in New Jersey and they have had their first child, Stephen.

"You'll be glad to know that I was able to nurse Stephen. You said you didn't know if I could and I am so pleased I can, and so is Stephen ..."

I have a clear image of Betsy and her medical problem, but sometimes my inability to recognize patients immediately and recall their names embarrasses me and wounds them. If I once did something important in their life, they will probably conclude that I never really cared much about them.

The fact is that at the time when I was the patient's surgeon, he or she did mean a great deal to me. My problem is I tend to forget names, or more precisely, I have never spent the effort to remember them initially. Since I have long had this mental lapse, I probably will not notice the condition worsening when I become senile.

I rationalize, however, that many patients do not want me to recognize them in public because of the intimate service I perform for them. They are fortunate that I have a built-in mechanism for preserving confidentiality.

To receive a photograph of a newborn from one parent whom I have known as a patient, as happened with Betsy MacGinnis, is not unusual. Recently, however, a baby picture came from two people whom I knew before they married and became parents. Each had had the same operation: a rhinoplasty and a chin implant. Although my office is hardly a romantic setting, their love began here. In fact, Joan and Mel invited me to their wedding, but I was in Europe.

The unusual circumstances of Joan's courtship alone would make her unforgettable, but I remember her first visit mainly because of her mother. She was a very dominating woman who had the fear that I would give her daughter a nose that looked "artificial, like a pig's snout."

"You know, I always can recognize someone who has had her nose done. They have a certain look."

For her generation, Joan's mother was correct, since many patients had what I would call a "signature nose," a rhinoplasty that was specific for the surgeon even if it was not appropriate for the patient. Now we try to be subtle, although we cannot guarantee that the patient will have a natural nose. The objective, at least for me, is to improve something by changing it so that it blends with the person.

As I looked at the picture of their new baby, I wondered whether Joan and Mel had secretly expected Lamarkian inheritance to work for them, so that the new baby would have an adequate chin and a good-looking nose. Would sexual selection be different, and natural selection also, if other forms of life, not just human beings, could have their own plastic surgeons?

11:15. Mrs. Edwards brings in her daughter, Edwina. I now feel the effort to peak for each patient. No rest in the turnstile.

I recall a writer in his sixties whom I saw a few years ago, at the end of a day that seemed to have forty-eight hours. His problem was a benign growth of his scalp. I was played out. My interaction with him was all form, no content. Even though I realized the hollowness of the consultation, I could not vitalize it. Like the marathoner, I just didn't have it that day. I felt like a mechanical hockey player in a game that we used to play as kids by moving the stick left or right to hit the oncoming ball. If we were skilled, the figure did the job well but never with emotion.

A few months after his last office visit, to my chagrin, I met the writer at someone's birthday party. The host was delighted that we already knew each other, the writer having made that disclosure. When he was asked how I took care of him, he replied, "Adequately." Being a writer and an honest one, he chose the right word. I deserved no better. I was a talking, doing doctor but, to him, not a living, caring physician. He would be surprised, I suspect, to find out that I cared more than he thought.

Mrs. Edwards is a well-dressed, stunning woman in her fifties, on whom I have done an eyelidplasty. I have never seen her daughter before. Edwina is sixteen, tall, with long hair that falls on a plain white blouse. She is wearing non-designer jeans. She radiates the energy and wholesomeness one might expect from an ardent equestrienne.

Edwina's surgical problem began when she was very young, about two years of age. She pulled a percolator of hot coffee from the stove and burned herself extensively on the chest. She required several weeks in the hospital and three skin-grafting procedures. Her mother still feels guilty for not having prevented the accident.

Edwina's breast development has been normal, but the upper part of her chest and breasts are very scarred. She dreads the summer, when she would like to wear bathing suits but does not. Since she is beginning to date, she fears intimacy. The stable and her horses provide refuge and solace as well as a hobby, I surmise.

I am not the only plastic surgeon that the Edwards family has consulted. The others have told her that very little can be done because, even if the scar is replaced with another skin graft, there is no predicting the final appearance of the eventual scar, which could be even worse than what she has now. Furthermore, they have said there will be a scar where the graft would be taken.

With this kind of history, I spend considerable time with a patient because I can probably offer nothing substantial. After inquiring about her school, summer plans, and her next horse show, I lead her to the examining room.

Unfortunately, the other plastic surgeons are correct. I do not advise further treatment. To tell her this is not easy. I do so as gently as possible after she has dressed and returned to the consulting room where her mother is waiting. We are a sad group. Edwina sobs. A sudden idea causes her to raise her head. She has heard of collagen injections.

"Would these help?" she asks.

"No, unfortunately. For thick scars, they are not indicated. Even for acne scars or aging wrinkles, when collagen is used, the long-term results are only fair, at best. The collagen is a foreign protein, from cows, and most patients need repeated injections."

Mrs. Edwards has found out that I have been doing some research on a "skin equivalent," in association with Professor Eugene Bell at the Massachusetts Institute of Technology. Our work, which holds promise, has not progressed to the point that we could replace her daughter's skin. At this stage, the skin equivalent we are making from the patient's own skin lacks normal pigment. I tell Edwina that I shall keep her name on file should something new come forth. I emphasize to her and her mother that medical science is advancing. Perhaps there will be a helpful discovery.

While it is important to offer hope, she must adapt to the reality of living with this problem, certainly for several years, and most likely forever. I invite her and her family to call me should they hear about a possible treatment. I say this because *The New York Times* or *Newsweek* may contain information long before it appears in one of our medical journals. I want Edwina to know that she can get in touch with me herself without fearing that I will be annoyed.

Since Edwina has seen other doctors, I do not recommend further consultations. I would do so if I had been the only physician that they had consulted. In that situation, the purpose of referrals is not only to be sure that I am right but also to be certain that the patient feels satisfied that she or he has explored every possibility.

I instruct Edwina or her mother to call me in six months so that I can give an update on my own research. To leave a patient totally without hope is another serious error. There is a story about Dr. Cecil Loeb, who used to be chief of medicine at Columbia-Presbyterian Hospital. Once, when he questioned a student who had examined a patient with cancer, Dr. Loeb asked him what he had said to that man. The student replied, "I told him, of course, that he had cancer."

"Did you tell him anything else?" Dr. Loeb asked.

"No."

Dr. Loeb thereupon ordered the student to leave the class and informed him that he would expel him from school. Dr. Loeb's stature was such that this was a reality, not just a threat. Painfully, the student made his way to the back of the amphitheater while the others sat shocked. As he reached the door, Dr. Loeb called him back with these words: "I want you to know how it feels to be all alone."

Those of us who are fortunate not to be marred externally have little idea of what others go through each day, each hour, even minute by minute. One patient, half the side of whose face I had removed because of a sarcoma and later reconstructed, remarked, "Going to the supermarket is like making it to the Olympics."

While it is true that when it comes to a disfigurement, society today is "more understanding" compared to a few decades ago—a phrase I use with patients—the fact is that most people cannot control their initial reaction of revulsion to the facially deformed. Even though they may say nothing, their faces register everything.

Darkness is the ally of the deformed. Some have told me that they count the hours until the lights go out, when they will be like everyone else. Some of the patients have solitary night jobs, a watchman or telephone operator. Although many, with effort, find another person to love, some do not. One of my patients, an unmarried forty-year-old man who has extensive, bulky tumors of his face (neurofibromatosis) wistfully observed: "All it takes is to get one person to love me and that should get me through life."

The modern age, while providing some medical and surgical help for the deformed, has stressed them in other ways. Electricity has done away with the sanctuary of the pitchy nights of the ancients. Clothing styles now expose more of the body. The veiled women in Kuwait are more fortunate than those in our country, who cannot easily hide deformity or aging.

Deformity isolates. Many physicians run away from those aspects of a patient's life with the excuse that the information is hard to elicit. But most patients need the opportunity to express their concerns.

For a woman who has had a mastectomy, for example, the sexual act is important, perhaps more so than it ever was. She wants to know whether someone will desire her physically.

A female psychiatrist told me after I had given a lecture on breast reconstruction that she urges women who have had a mastectomy to resume sex immediately. In her words, "The longer they wait, the harder the emotional recovery."

I remember a woman who came to me for reconstruction of both breasts. Eighteen years before, she had her first radical mastectomy. This was the classic Halsted operation, which took the breast and the underlying muscle and so much skin that she needed a graft to her right chest, which when I saw her looked like a washboard. Later, because of cancer of the other breast, she had another radical mastectomy, but this one spared some of the pectoral muscle and was done without a graft. While she was changing in the examining room, her husband, a strong farmer, started to cry and said that their life together for the past eighteen years had been "a secret hell." They already had their children and tried to create the semblance of a close family, but, in his words, "It has hung over us—all these years."

Tolstoy supposedly said to Gorky, "Of all human tragedies, the worst is that of the bedroom."

What was unfortunate, even reprehensible, about the patient's situation was that the doctor who did the mastectomies never asked her about her relationship with her husband, specifically about their sexual life. Admittedly, as mentioned, these facts are not usually on the surface, and many years ago people felt inhibited to discuss them and doctors more inhibited to ask them. Yet any physician who does breast surgery should be interested in a patient's rehabilitation, emotional as well as physical. Spending twenty minutes with a patient aiding her to recover normal arm motion is important, but so is an assessment of functioning in another crucial area of her life.

I referred this woman, who was from Texas, to a colleague near her home because it would be more convenient and less costly than journeying back and forth to Boston. She had her reconstruction—both breasts—and I understand from her surgeon that she and her husband are having a better life together.

With that woman and with almost all patients, hard as I try, I can't always feel what they are experiencing. The only time I was a patient in my own field of plastic and reconstructive surgery was when I was a resident and had a mole removed from my face. Though it looked benign, I anxiously waited for the pathologist's report. When I learned that it was not a melanoma, I wanted to celebrate but I never did because of the pressure of work.

I have had, however, some illnesses and their resultant operations: appendicitis, appendectomy; tonsillitis, tonsillectomy—all when I was very young. Much later, when I was with Dr. Schweitzer in Africa, I noted a scaliness of my legs and scalp after having been there only three weeks. No one, including Dr. Schweitzer, knew the cause. Only after I returned home was the diagnosis of psoriasis made. The onset, it was felt, came after my taking an antimalarial drug. I did have a genetic predisposition, since a maternal aunt had rheumatoid arthritis and the relationship between this collagen disease and psoriasis is well known. I recall her valiant but futile fight against the deformity that ultimately left her helpless in bed.

My psoriasis responds easily to coal tar and sun. Nevertheless, it is an incurable nuisance, and I can understand the momentary ecstasy that comes to patients when they dream that they have been freed of a disease. More of an optimist than a pessimist, I was not prepared for the disagreeable turn my psoriasis took. In fact, I should have known I was developing arthritis because of the increasing stiffness of my joints and my losing weight despite my eating more. That the psoriasis was also worsening I conveniently overlooked until one of my toes swelled. My wife, a psychiatric social worker without medical training but with common sense, told me one evening that she had diagnosed my problem as psoriatic arthritis. She reached this conclusion after looking through one of my textbooks. At that time I was the attending plastic surgeon at the Robert Breck Brigham Hospital, which was devoted solely to collagen diseases. I informed my wife that I, not she, should know whether I had psoriatic arthritis. Nevertheless, I did go to a physician, who told me without hesitation that my wife was absolutely correct.

That I now had to confront a potentially deforming disease shocked me. I remembered only my aunt and the unfortunate patients whose extremities, particularly the hands, psoriatic arthritis had crippled. This thought depressed me greatly, since it could mean the end of my being a surgeon. To take surgery away from a surgeon is emasculation. When my doctor pointed out that patients hospitalized with psoriatic arthritis constituted only a small percentage of those who had it, it comforted me, but only a little. I minded the disease but even more the label. From a rational point of view, I was still the same person twenty-four hours after the diagnosis as I was before. Yet I could not shake myself free of the branding, the stigma.

I have never forgotten that episode, particularly when I must tell a patient that he or she has cancer. I remember distinctly how depressed I was for a few days when I thought I detected signs and symptoms of arthritis in my hands. In actuality, none existed. As a matter of fact, the condition has not affected my hands except for a transient ache or swelling in one thumb if I do very heavy lifting. My malady has never interfered with my operating schedule. In those dark days, however, I was not easy to live with; finally my wife called my doctor. She told him that I was planning not to return to work for a few weeks, even though this was not the advice that he had given me. He quickly ordered me to resume my normal schedule. How well he understood me! He also cheered me by citing Oliver Wendell Holmes's formula for longevity: "Have a chronic disease and take care of it."

From my illness I learned another lesson about the needs of patients.

I was happy to have my wife take over, glad to be the

recipient in her maternal role. Although I knew from what I had been taught in medical school and from what I had seen in practice that patients wish to be cared for, I had not realized its truth and my need. I understood better also how overwhelming sickness and dependency can be to someone who is usually so active and accustomed to helping others. Never having been psychoanalyzed, I do not know whether I am active and giving because I truly am or, in fact, I am really the opposite. Does it matter so long as one functions effectively at a level appropriate for the occasion?

Another illness taught me something about what it is like to be a patient in a hospital. A kidney stone disrupted a beautiful August night. Again my behavior proved the wisdom of the adage that a doctor who treats himself has a fool for a patient. Although I had the classic symptoms and signs of a renal calculus, I could not bring myself to make the diagnosis. I was consciously reluctant to give myself another illness—which, despite my training and profession, I consider a taint. I never deem illness to be so in my patients, to whom I frequently say, "It's a law of nature and life: all of us get sick. It's nobody's fault. It's just being human." Yet, when it happened to me, I felt ashamed of being defective.

On the occasion of my kidney stone, I had enough sense to call a physician who advised me to go to the hospital, where I passed the pebble—a feeling akin to giving birth to an elk.

Over the next few years I had two more episodes and the last required admission. I ended up in a room where, twelve hours before, I had been a consultant to the patient in the next bed. Illness is mindless and does not distinguish between those with medical degrees and those without.

That hospitalization, though it only lasted for a day and a half since I was fortunate to get rid of the stone, enlightened me further about the role of the patient. I went to the X-ray department, and there I had a severe attack of renal colic. The secretary, like a good bureaucrat, was interested more in my papers than in my pain and totally ignored me. Finally, someone who was with another patient waiting for her X rays came over and said, "I heard you being called 'doctor.' It must be very difficult for you as a doctor to be a patient, and I am sorry that you're having so much pain." That woman, whom I did not know and have never seen since, found the essence of medicine. While one cannot do something for a patient, one should always try to empathize with the suffering.

Being a physician and the son of a physician, I have spent most of my life taking doctors for granted. I was surprised at the mental relief that came when my urologist entered my room. Without doubt, the presence of a good and sympathetic doctor does make a significant difference. The pain from the kidney stone and, a few years later, pain from a partially herniated disc made me an unwilling expert on physical anguish.

I learned that another major factor in how we deal with pain is its predictability or unpredictability. Not knowing when "it"—the "enemy"—will strike increases anxiety and worsens pain.

When I had my kidney stone, for example, I used to imagine that the calculus was the ironclad *Monitor* ready to sail my inner waterway. Since I never knew when the next attack would begin, the intervals between bombardments were never tranquil. In contrast, when I once had an episode of spinal nerve-root pain, I could accurately gauge its onset and duration since specific movements set it off. Yet, because I did not know when I would eventually get better, I still suffered from the ambiguity. However, I did assume, correctly, that I would again be well—unlike some of my unfortunate patients with cancer who have to bear not only the pain but the knowledge that they are incurable.

How insensitive we physicians must appear to patients in pain, I realized, even those of us who are supposedly caring doctors. We blithely expect patients to "function," to be "brave," and to be "cooperative, good patients."

Pain is an enervator; it induces overwhelming fatigue that finally brings on sleep, the welcomed anodyne.

In the midst of pain, I remember my wondering how a part of myself could wage war against me. Again, the perennial questions of the sufferer: Why me? Why this illness?

Pain has another sinister effect: it turns self into self. The global view disappears. Who can think cosmically when a kidney stone is sailing on your Grand Canal? Your world contracts faster than the speed of light. The planet becomes a one-by-one-millimeter pebble. You cannot resist becoming the bore, venting to any listener your confrontation with pain or, more accurately, your bare-knuckled fight. You recount it with a memory of the unpleasantness of a bad dream but also with satisfaction, if you successfully passed the inner test. Loved ones soon tire of your corporeal fixation, your compulsive recitation of the nuances of what was one of your few authentic, core experiences. They listen because they owe you an obligation from days that were better, without pain.

Everyone has an inner list of maladies that he or she

expects to sustain in a lifetime, and almost every patient whom I have questioned is unambiguous about which one he or she expects will be the fatal force. The chronic smoker expects to die of lung cancer, but if it is to be death from malignant melanoma, he will likely resent the betrayal. Most of us have not accepted death as part of our life plan. If the assassin is totally unanticipated, we become even more indignant at the intrusion.

Even a physician who has been ill, however, cannot comprehend, when he is in good health, what it is to be a patient. How can a male physician properly understand, for example, such a common event as menstrual cramps? Does a thirty-five-year-old doctor truly know the mind of an eighty-year-old man facing death? It is easy to be there, but from a distance. In truth, for most of our lives, whether we are doctors or not, we are tourists passing through the lives of others.

chapter 6

During my early years in practice, I became increasingly aware that many of my surgical results were not so good as those shown at meetings or published in articles. I naturally assumed that these shortcomings were due to my inexperience. While my being a neophyte was undoubtedly responsible for some undistinguished results, I soon concluded, after speaking to senior colleagues, that they also had the same problems. This realization prompted me to edit a book, *The Unfavorable Result in Plastic Surgery: Avoidance and Treatment.* At first, many prospective authors were reluctant to contribute chapters, because they feared they would become known more for their failures than their feats. Others were enthusiastic. For them, a public admission of suboptimal surgical outcomes might have been a welcomed catharsis.

I was careful in the title of my book when I chose the word "unfavorable," since in plastic surgery many patients have objectionable results that are not such frank complications as infection, bleeding, or death. A tip of a nose, for example, that appears pinched after rhinoplasty is an unfavorable result. It is not as significant a complication as would be a pulmonary embolism following an operation. That disaster is the kind discussed in the hospital at weekly "morbidity and mortality" rounds. I also soon realized that an objectively excellent surgical result is not always synonymous with an ecstatic patient. Some patients may be disappointed for many reasons, not all of them having to do with the anatomic change after surgery.

My next patient this morning, Dr. Shapiro, illustrates this situation. As he comes through the door, I sigh inwardly. He is a thirty-eight-year-old psychologist, on whom I should not have done a rhinoplasty. I now admit that I knew before I operated that he might be a dissatisfied patient, but I ignored all the warnings. Male rhinoplasty patients are notorious for their high rate of unhappiness with the result, no matter how good it may appear to somebody else. A male over thirty who comes for a cosmetic rhinoplasty without ever having had injury is, in my experience, likely to be an unhappy patient. Usually he is single, solitary, and may be homosexual or valiantly bisexual. While his sexual preferences do not really concern me, his emotional reactions to his surgery do.

For males, the nose supposedly has a strong sexual significance. In men the nose is the only projecting midline structure other than the penis. Since the older male rhinoplasty patient is likely to have a problem with sexual identification, there is a dilemma for him and me because he does not know, nor do I, how male or female he wants his new nose to be. When some of these patients have brought me photographs of the kind of nose they want, the picture has often been that of a female.

A common complaint of male patients after operation is that the nose is still too large. While it is possible that a patient may be correct, usually his evaluation has little anatomical justification. If the surgeon, trying to anticipate that reaction, were to whittle away the nose with abandon, it might be too small, too pinched. The criticism then would probably be, "You made me look like a girl." At a conscious level they do not like that, even though it might please them unconsciously. I admit that I have always tried to avoid the situation of doing too much. If I have erred, it is usually on the side of masculinity. Perhaps I have been wrong, but I do not want to put a "female" nose on a male, especially a nose that would not be pleasing even to a female. Perhaps also a female plastic surgeon or one who is a homosexual might have a different experience with these male patients, who might be happier in their hands.

A year has passed since Dr. Shapiro's operation. Although he had a mildly deviated septum, his purpose in having the procedure was not to breathe better but to look better, whatever that meant to him. As so often happens with male rhinoplasty patients, his result would be judged by most to be very good, but for him it has not been good enough. When he saw me last, he said, "Please don't misunderstand me, doctor, I am grateful for what you have done because it is a significant improvement, but I really think that, if it were less full at the tip, it would look so much better."

"As I told you, Dr. Shapiro," I now said to him, "I think that the nose fits your face. If the tip were narrowed, it might have a pinched, artificial appearance."

"Would you try to do a little more?"

I feel myself weakening under the pressure that he is applying. In such a situation, I try to arrange a consultation with somebody else, who might appraise him anew with more objectivity. If that surgeon were to undertake the operation, he would do it, I hope, with more confidence than I can muster. Dr. Shapiro is still in psychotherapy as part of his training, and I ask him what his analyst thinks.

"He said that you and I should discuss it, and if I felt that I could be improved and you felt that you could improve me, then we should go ahead with it."

I expected this circumspect statement. After much discussion, Dr. Shapiro agrees to see another plastic surgeon whose name I have given him. In these circumstances, the patient must not feel that the surgeon is jettisoning him but directing him. That is sometimes hard to do because the surgeon may be relieved to see that patient exit from his office and his life. I confess that I would not be disappointed if Dr. Shapiro went somewhere else.

It is important for a plastic surgeon to have a consultant he or she respects and can trust. There are many plastic surgeons who will unconsciously or consciously worsen the relationship between the patient and the referring doctor. They feed off the misery of others. It is possible to be truthful with the patient, and yet disagree with the referring doctor, while also maintaining whatever good ties exist between the unhappy patient and the stressed surgeon.

Fortunately, at least externally, Dr. Shapiro seems more disappointed than angry. Perhaps his hostility will burst forth as his therapy progresses. But, at this point, I am lucky that he is not openly aggressive, since one of my weaknesses is that I cannot handle anger easily. I do not like expressing my own or receiving someone else's. I admire psychiatrists who deal regularly with aggression without becoming murderously responsive or demurely retiring. Most doctors, and perhaps especially only children, have the Good Boy or Good Girl syndrome. We lust for approbation. Plastic surgeons seem to have an inordinate need for immediate gratification. Although we depend upon wound-healing, which takes several months to produce the final result, we have a reasonable idea of the outcome by the end of the operation or within a few weeks. Since our work is an extension of ourselves, when a patient, even with merit, does not like what we have done, we wrongly consider it a personal indictment and react defensively.

Plastic surgeons realize that the body belongs to the patient, but in one sense they have an investment in it. Admittedly, this proprietary attitude is unreasonable, since we are expropriating from the patient what is not ours. Yet sometimes the blurring of boundaries between the province of patient and physician is beneficial and is evidence of the doctor's commitment to and involvement with the person who comes for help.

When dealing with the patient who is dissatisfied because of a complication, the surgeon must learn to separate himself from the anatomic problem. With Dr. Shapiro, I do not flagellate myself. I feel that I have done what most would consider a technically satisfactory job. I recognize that I should not have undertaken the procedure, but while I erred in patient selection, I did not make a mistake in the operation itself, despite the patient's feeling that the tip of the nose should have been smaller. I shall be supportive of Dr. Shapiro. The ball is in his court. He, more than I, must adjust to the reality. Perhaps after he sees another plastic surgeon, there will be a different reality for us, but I do not believe he needs someone to do something to his nose; he needs to do more work on himself with his therapist.

After Dr. Shapiro leaves, another patient takes his place in my mind. It is Mrs. Julia Evans, who wrote me last week that she still has tightness and pain in her neck following a facelift I did for her four years ago. Would that I could become inured to her complaints! I cannot even get angry at her, since the reality is that I, with my operation, brought about her problem and our burden.

Mrs. Julia Evans was then a sixty-nine-year-old widow. She had worked many years as supervisor of a school cafeteria. What she earned had supplemented her husband's salary as a building inspector in Boston. They had a son who had been in the air force but had died in a plane crash several years before I saw her.

The reason Mrs. Evans consulted me for a facelift was to "get back to work, to do something instead of just staying at home."

She was the kind of elderly lady who dresses meticulously, conservatively. Her dark blue suit went well with her white hair, navy shoes, blue eyes, and Celtic complexion. She wore earrings and a brooch and carried a handbag the color of which matched her shoes.

To me, she seemed a straightforward patient whose appearance I could improve greatly because she had markedly redundant skin of her upper lids, cheeks, and neck. Under her chin, she also had a lot of fat that I planned to remove.

When she entered the hospital, the day before her operation, the resident asked me, "Why are you doing her?"

His question jolted me.

"Why do you ask me that?" I queried.

"She seems sad and lost," he replied.

When I saw her in the room, she did appear subdued, a mood I ascribed to her apprehension about the operation.

She and I discussed the procedure once again, and at no time did I detect anything unusual, other than her quiet manner.

Technically her operation "went well," the surgeon's usual phrase for a procedure without complications. Her hospital course was also "uneventful," another word we use when the patient and the surgeon are fortunate.

The problem of pain began three weeks after her surgery, a week after I had taken out her stitches. Patients may complain of numbness, stiffness, and pain in their neck, especially if they have had their superficial muscle (the platysma) tightened and divided. I had done this in Mrs. Evans and had also defatted her neck.

Mrs. Evans's complaints, I thought, were due to these aspects of her operation. However, the pain persisted for many months.

Occasionally, the cause may be a neuroma, a clump of painful nerve endings, which might have resulted in her case from cutting a sensory nerve. But I could not feel a nodule or lump that might indicate a neuroma. I referred Mrs. Evans to a neurologist, then a neurosurgeon, but they also found nothing anatomic to explain her symptoms: no neuroma, no nerve-root pain (cervical radiculitis), no foreign body such as an imbedded suture.

I then had to conclude that her pain was most likely psychogenic, a suspicion that I had earlier but did not want to offer until I thought I had excluded everything else. Even a neurotic must die of something specific.

The psychiatrist who saw her thought Mrs. Evans was depressed. He traced its etiology to an unresolved grief reaction over the death of her son. In fact, as we later found out, Mrs. Evans had scheduled her facelift on the fourth anniversary of his death.

Perhaps, when she realized after the operation that, even with her improved looks, her life and its sadness would not change, she became even more depressed. The resident was more acute than I in perceiving her despondency preoperatively.

I should add that Mrs. Evans's commemorative surgery is not unique. I have had several women who scheduled their reduction mammoplasty or a facelift to coincide with the date of their husband's death. In every instance, the husband had opposed the surgery. Their having the operation was an act of liberation and of defiance.

Mrs. Evans, fortunately, improved with antidepressants, psychotherapy, and time. Although her symptoms have not disappeared, they have lost their intensity. I saw her on a weekly basis and was soon able to extend the interval to every two weeks, then to every month. Between appointments, she would call to let me know that she still had pain.

"Doctor, it's still there," she would say, but not with the same anguish.

I noticed also that, whenever she visited her sister in Connecticut, her pain vanished. My explanation for this phenomenon was that she was less lonely with her sister, but her reasoning was that "it's warmer in Connecticut, farther south, and heat helps my neck."

The letter that I just received from Mrs. Evans does not surprise me, since she and I regularly keep in touch. The routine is that, when I hear from her, I write her to ask that she make an appointment to see me in the office. She does, and we talk. Our relationship now has a minuet quality.

Not every patient with puzzling pain after a facelift is necessarily someone that one should have avoided surgically. I would still have operated on Emma Olmstead. I don't know how she is faring now, since I have not heard from her in a couple of years. She would write at Christmas in green ink with her distinctive, elaborate script that resembled calligraphy. Her cards were her own creation. She had studied in Boston at the Museum of Fine Arts more than forty years ago. When I first met her, she was fifty-seven. She was then working in a gallery on Newbury Street. After she retired, Emma returned to Maine to the home where she was born, and which she inherited when her mother died. Emma had never married and told me that she liked traveling too much to renounce her independence.

When I first saw her in my office, what impressed me was her appearance: a melding of the young and the old. Of average height but slender and graceful, one could easily mistake her from the back for a twenty-five-year-old, were it not for her long white hair held by a massive barrette of old Dutch silver.

Emma had the look of slight disorder that seemed to go with her artistic background. It fitted also with her liberal political views and her zeal to save dolphins, whales, and anything else Noah had put in his ark.

Her skin was Nordic, without blemish, except for wrinkles beginning to course her upper lip. Her upper lids had heavy hoods. She objected to them, as well as to the jowls and the loose skin of her neck. She was very direct about her reason for facial surgery. "Just because I'm retired, I don't want to look old. I want to make a fresh start again."

She underwent a facelift, upper eyelidplasty, and a chemical peel, using phenol, on the upper lip. Her operation and recovery were uncomplicated and her result, she and I thought, superior.

A year later, she called to say that something was troubling her: pain in the incision behind her right ear.

When I examined her, the scar looked normal. It was not thick; the wound had healed without infection and without any evidence of remnant suture.

"This pain keeps me up at night," she said, and, indeed, she looked as if she had not been sleeping well. She had lost her verve and now seemed like any distraught woman leaving a supermarket on a Saturday morning with her grandchildren.

If I had been a psychiatrist, I would have been more subtle. However, thirty years in surgery, counting my residency, is poor preparation for a casual entry.

"Tell me, Miss Olmstead, has anything different happened in your life within the past few months?"

She stared at me, raised her hands, let them fall helplessly into her lap, and lowered her head and sobbed. What she told me explained her problem but did not offer a solution.

For the past thirty-five years, she had been the acknowledged mistress of a well-known politician. In the summers, she had even accompanied him and his family wherever they went. During the year, she lived close to his home in an apartment that her friend had provided. I wondered whether he treated her with the same lack of largesse that Victor Hugo had shown his mistress, Juliette Drouet.

A month ago, her friend felt unusually tired, and cancer of the colon was found. He was to have an operation. She told me her "terrible fear" that he was going to die and that she would be completely alone.

"I guess you are the only person that I can speak to, since I really have been so healthy that I don't have a family doctor and I don't even belong to a church."

I gently pointed out to her the relationship between the pain around her ear and what was happening to the most important person in her life. She left feeling better but obviously concerned. About two weeks later, she called to tell me that her friend's operation had been successful. The cancer had been taken out, and as far as the doctors could determine, the tumor had not spread to the lymph nodes. His prognosis, according to the surgeon, was excellent. Before she hung up, she added that the pain behind her ear had gone away.

About a year ago, I read that her lover had died. I suppose she went to the funeral, since the wife had tolerated her presence while he was alive. Maybe they were once enemies, but I have the fantasy they have since become friends, both having been exploited and abandoned by the same man.

With a patient who is dissatisfied, the hardest burden for me is the realization that I didn't perform an operation well. In my practice, bad mistakes are rare; yet perfection is rarer still. Unlike other surgeons who can cover an error with skin, we plastic surgeons cannot. Our slip-ups are self-evident. One does not have to be a plastic surgeon or even a doctor to know that less or more should have been done.

The latter is true for the next patient, Mrs. Fay Levy, who always arrives promptly. Six weeks ago, she had a facelift, but she still has a small area of fat that I should have taken away when I thinned her neck. This fullness upsets her, and my plan is to wait for the tissues to heal and then to remove the extra fat under local anesthesia on an outpatient basis. I have told her also that I will not charge her. Some surgeons, however, do make the patient pay an additional fee, so that the patient or an attorney cannot say that the surgeon, by not charging, is admitting negligence. My belief is that forcing the patient to pay more for finishing the job is provocative, to say the least. I know how I would react if a carpenter charged me again for work that he should have done adequately the first time. (Some of my colleagues would protest that we are not carpenters.)

I believe it is important to be honest with the patient when something has gone wrong. The worst error is not to admit that anything is awry. I recall a patient who had a reduction mammoplasty that left her nipples asymmetrical. The surgeon responsible told her that they were "normal" or "close to normal." Distorting reality to the doctor's advantage is really no advantage. It further injures the patient, who resents being treated like a child, and a stupid one at that.

A surgeon who is willing to admit that something is not right, sympathizes with the patient, and knows what to do next can sometimes convert a disaster into victory. Both doctor and patient can emerge satisfied, if not ecstatic.

Another major mistake for the surgeon is to become angry at the unhappy patient, as if he or she is responsible for what has happened or for what the surgeon may have done poorly. To become distant or unavailable is unwise and unfair. Admittedly, most of us like to flee from defeat. The plastic surgeon who is used to success must guard against a flight reaction, since running away is a natural and life-saving response to an unpleasant situation. I remember as a child of ten hitting a baseball that broke a neighbor's window. We all fled home. My mother, sensing that something had gone wrong, easily extracted the truth. She made me return to the neighbor's house and wait until he came home. When I told him the circumstances of his broken window and offered to pay for its replacement, he fortunately was not only understanding but surprised at my honesty. Whenever I have the temptation to dodge or hide something professionally, that incident remains a strict reminder.

The aesthetic surgeon, who deals in happiness, lives unconsciously by a simplistic equation: A good operation equals a happy patient. We are warmed by the eternal flame of praise, expecting a patient whose looks we have improved to extol us. Genuflection is admittedly passé unless a pope or monarch is around, but the plastic surgeon, especially someone young, expects a profusion of superlatives from the patient. Soon he learns to settle for a minimum of complaints and a paid bill. Later the surgeon is happy if a patient doesn't become a malpractice threat.

Even though Mrs. Levy will not have to pay me for further surgery, she will have to take care of the hospital costs. All my patients prior to operation must sign a form that holds them responsible for hospital charges associated with improving a result or treating a complication. For eighteen years in practice, I resisted having such forms, since they seem too starkly financial and cold. I am still uncomfortable when I get into the realm of money, more uneasy than in any other aspect of a patient's treatment.

Mrs. Fay Levy, who is fifty-eight, is scowling this morning. Her glance could turn a cucumber into a pickle. Her displeasure offsets the improvement that the facelift has given her despite the fact that a small one-by-one-inch area of fat remains in her upper neck, under the chin, slightly to the left of the midline. With her brown hair, freed of gray by an attentive hairdresser, her antique gold necklace and earrings, and her conservative, well-tailored clothes, she is not someone one might expect to take this problem lightly.

Mrs. Levy, like most of us confronting unpleasantness, perseveres in wonder. "How did this happen?"

I invoke human error.

"Why didn't you get rid of this lump at the time of operation?"

I explain again that I had not realized during her surgery that this little piece of fat was there, since the dissection was extensive and the swelling at operation considerable.

"You might know that something like this would happen to me," she mourns, feeling victimized, though her dress and bearing do not suggest a victim. Yet female patients, more than male, articulate their sense of being exploited, and perhaps that reaction is not unjustified, considering the socioeconomic realities of our society. And Mrs. Levy has reason for complaint with respect to males. Two years ago her husband left her for one of her friends—a double betrayal. Perhaps she thinks that what I did to her is more treachery.

I try to enlarge her perspective. "After all, this is not a major complication, just a very small amount of fat that can be removed simply on an outpatient basis. You don't even need to go to the main operating room."

Mrs. Levy grudgingly accepts the need for the "touch-up," a euphemism we plastic surgeons find useful to designate another procedure undertaken to improve the first.

For the patient and the surgeon it is therapeutic to have a plan and to state it. I tell Mrs. Levy that I can operate again, but she has to wait for complete wound-healing, and that will take another three months. It is harmful to the patient and the family, as well as to the surgeon, to flounder in ambiguity. A semblance of structure may be structure enough in a case like this. With a measured voice, I say: "What we have to do is to wait for four months, and then your healing will have progressed to the point where we can easily do this minor procedure." Mrs. Levy nods.

It would have been an error to have said, "I guess we should wait a little while and then consider doing something. Maybe in a month, or two months, or maybe longer."

My secretary gives Mrs. Levy another office appointment in three weeks. It is very important to see an unhappy patient frequently. If not, the patient will become more despondent and will think poorly of you because you have abandoned him or her, and you will think poorly of yourself because it is true.

I walk Mrs. Levy to the door, a small courtesy, and say good-bye. I do not address her or any adult patient by their first name unless the patient requests it or permits it after I have asked their feelings about it. Perhaps decades are showing, but I am uncomfortable when a patient whom I have never met before first-names me. Although some patients feel more secure with a doctor who uses their first name, others may regard it as unwanted familiarity and a disquieting reminder of their medical dependency.

Also, women today are particularly sensitive to a male doctor's patronizing attitude that treats them as children. My being careful about calling a female patient by her first name is also less threatening to her male intimate—if she has one—who may think that I am trying to usurp his position. He may already be hostile because he has long opposed her surgical plans.

Unlike Mrs. Levy, some patients become depressed after a facelift or an eyelidplasty, even when the result is good. Early in practice the plastic surgeon is emotionally unprepared for managing those transient doldrums that usually are not so profound that they require psychotherapy and medication. Although premenstrual tension may cause or aggravate the depression, it can happen to women who have long passed their menopause. The dip in the emotions is due partly to the withdrawal of cortisone secreted in response to the operation and its associated stresses. But a major and obvious cause of the depression is the patient's appearance immediately after surgery. She is usually black and blue and has marked swelling, which hides and distorts the improvement that was visible even when she was on the operating room table. The patient also may have secretly expected to look younger and more beautiful than she ever admitted to the surgeon and even to herself, and she may have wanted that transformation to be instantaneous. The plastic surgeon, who thinks that he has done a good job, may become angry at her because of her unrealistic expectations. He may chide her for her impatience, saying, "Remember, I told you that you would be black and blue and swollen and you would have to wait a few weeks before seeing the improvement."

The genesis of the depression may be the cruel overwhelming realization that, although her face may soon look better, her life will likely stay the same: a monotonous marriage, a wayward child, a dying parent, an enervating job—and in this world it is possible for one person to have more than a single misfortune.

For the patient, it is less important to have a surgeon who is right about what he told her preoperatively than to have one who is right there, reassuring, supportive, and sympathetic. It is interesting that most male patients, though constituting only ten percent of those having cosmetic surgery, almost never experience this kind of depression. Indeed, they are at a greater disadvantage with respect to their postoperative appearance because they do not use makeup, which in women helps not only to restore normalcy but to avoid the relentless curiosity of friends and even strangers.

After eyelidplasty and facelift, more than with any other procedures in aesthetic surgery, the opinions of others greatly influence the patient's satisfaction or dissatisfaction with the anatomical outcome. The middle-aged woman is extremely vulnerable to the judgment of her friends, especially those of the same sex. Their approval or disapproval is more important than that of her husband. Because she may have undertaken her operation despite his opposition or with his grudging consent, his opinion is not now important since it never was. But even though she sought the operation by herself and presumably for herself, she is overly aware of the reactions of those around her. Just at the time she desperately wants support, her friends may impale her with their verbal thrusts.

"You really look funny."

"Your eyes don't match."

"You certainly are swollen. Will it ever go away under your chin?"

"How come Betty looks so much better than you, and you went to the same surgeon?" (Betty may be six months postoperative and this patient only three weeks.)

"I told you you should have gone to someone else."

"After seeing what you look like, I'd never have it done."

And the most savage of all, to the woman who had her surgery a few months before: "When are you going to have your facelift?"

That remark, which may be premeditated, is certain to send the patient whimpering back to my office to see her preoperative photographs. But even if the patient can perceive and acknowledge the improvement, the damage is done, and the verbal scar remains.

How apt the line from the Old Testament: "I was wounded in the house of my friends."

Having said all this, I cannot dodge the truth that for some patients a facelift, even if performed correctly, will not make a spectacular difference, and even if it does, it may not last more than a year or two. Time and gravity conquer all. In general, the worse the sagging, the more noticeable the improvement, and the longer its duration.

The plastic surgeon who believes in the preventive facelift runs the risk of having many patients whom they have helped only minimally. Doing a facelift before the patient really needs it is like painting a house every year when it does not visibly require a recoating. Unlike a wooden structure, however, a patient undertakes definite risks and gets permanent scars. She may have spent money saved for years only to get a disappointing result.

There are some patients who, though happy initially, become dissatisfied later and return, complaining that a wrinkle did not go away. Or they remark: "I know that I look better but I thought it would be much better." They say this despite all the disclaimers, verbal and written, that the plastic surgeon gave them.

I sense trouble when a patient replies to my question of "How are you doing?" with "You tell me, doctor." She is certain to be unhappy and may want not just to be reassured but also convinced, and that may be impossible to do.

With probing, the patient may then say, "I know your reputation and I realize that you did your best, but I am disappointed." This remark is the hardest for the plastic surgeon to bear. It is difficult to become angry at the patient who speaks the truth, even though you do not want to hear it. My reaction is one of guilt, which lingers longer than rage.

At that point in the conversation, the patient may ask to see her preoperative photographs, usually to show you that she is the same as she was prior to surgery. If you as the surgeon think that the operation has benefitted the patient, you may have already produced the pictures in order to convince her.

Whenever a dissatisfied patient asks for his or her photographs, a malpractice suit is hovering.

In Massachusetts, the law is explicit: photographs and records belong to the patient. The naive among us would assume that photographs show the reality. Indeed, they should, but it is possible to make the postoperative result look better depending upon how one takes the picture. As editor of a plastic surgical journal, I confront this chicanery frequently. The patient for a facelift may be told to flex her head for her preoperative photographs, since this accentuates the fat and folds under her chin. The postoperative views will look better if she holds her head slightly back, wears makeup, and is under a bright light.

A patient who is dissatisfied has another element to contend with: in my office, he or she is on my turf. The patient away from her familiar territory must conform to mine. That is one reason why we physicians get only a partial impression of every person coming to us. The family doctor who made house calls knew better what his patient and family were like. He saw where they lived and how they lived.

As much as I do not enjoy having a patient who is dissatisfied and angry at me, I can appreciate his or her vulnerability, especially away from home base.

Because cosmetic surgery may produce unhappiness, we have learned the wisdom of prepayment. Without insurance coverage for aesthetic procedures, having the patient pay the bill beforehand gives the surgeon his or her fee. The justification that we plastic surgeons offer ourselves is that studies have shown that patients who have already paid for an operation are generally more pleased with the result.

While this may or may not be true, what is incontestable is that the surgeon is happier for having received his wages, since many patients would not pay for an outcome that fell below their expectations. Indeed, perhaps because they have usually paid a considerable amount, they may feel the pressure to convince themselves and others that they are happy with what they have had done. The plastic surgeon who has an extensive cosmetic practice is never permitted to forget that he deals with happiness, as elusive as peace and immortality.

Cosmetic surgery is difficult less because of the technical demands than the personalities and expectations of many aesthetic surgical patients. If insurance covered the facelift, paid only $800, and prohibited additional charges, I doubt that most of us surgeons would do the operation with enthusiasm unless we were financially stressed. In general, patients whose complaints are of a more medical and reconstructive nature and therefore less cosmetic are easier to manage emotionally from the surgeon's point of view. Most plastic surgeons would agree privately, though not publicly, with this sentiment. They would not wish to lose the remunerative segment of their practice by failing to appear "understanding" and "compassionate," especially toward those with enviable incomes.

For the surgical resident rotating on the plastic service, it is a jolt to leave patients who complain of cancer pain to help those whose unhappiness comes from a sagging face. Unless the resident has a particular interest in plastic surgery, he or she reacts by thinking that these people are vain, selfish, narcissistic, and childish. Frequently they ask, "How do you put up with them?"

I remember a forty-year-old woman scheduled for a facelift who arrived in her hospital room just as I came to see her. She was to share it with an elderly patient in congestive heart failure who was receiving oxygen. My patient remarked as soon as she crossed the threshold, "My God, now I can't smoke."

Yet the same person in a different medical setting would likely behave as most do. The cosmetic patient has become so much a part of my daily landscape that usually I am not aware of what others might consider their shortcomings.

Perhaps it is too taxing for me to be judgmental, to categorize patients as good or bad. Furthermore, it is useless and even cruel to tell a patient who protests against a remaining wrinkle after a facelift that, in the next examining room, there is someone who has lost a breast or a cheek from cancer. I guarantee the response: "Oh! How terrible for her! I am so sorry, but getting back to me, why didn't this little puffy spot go away?"

It is also unreasonable to ask a patient to become cavalier about her face after a lift when, in fact, she came for the procedure because she was so conscious of it. I have never found the master spigot that turns on or off a patient's personality.

chapter 7

12:00. Now definitely behind. My secretary calls the operating room to tell them that I will be a half-hour late; fortunately, they are "delayed," a favorite word for a lagging schedule. The feeling of being crowded by patients is a natural state to me and to most practitioners. Sometimes, however, I would like to tell a patient, as did Jung: "Oh, no. I can't stand the sight of another one. Just go home and cure yourself today." I frequently have the fantasy that the Lord will slip in another day this week and get me back on schedule. Yet I know that any unscheduled time that came my way as a gift I would soon consume in tasks. I plead in my defense that it is not always my fault. There are unexpected patients, urgent problems. While that is true, another person less striving, less intense, innately perhaps more moderate, would plan for such happenings.

Since my patients know that I am not a psychiatrist

with a fixed hour per patient, they can take liberties with me. I radiate permission, and they sense that I am open-ended. Frequently a patient will talk about something that does not specifically concern the surgical problem. For example, a woman might say, "I am fine, but my husband is not." Certainly a physician under those circumstances should hear her out. I not only tacitly invite these revelations but, I confess, prompt them. I consciously fight the strictures of what could be a narrow specialty. I know what I am doing when I inquire, "Mrs. ———, how are things going, aside from where I have operated?" Although some patients remain noncommittal, others burst forth. It is hard to resist the request to be heard. The family doctor exists more in Rockwell's paintings than in real life today. Connections with the church are less close than they were. Divorce is common, and even those who are married are not usually coupled with their best friend. Families are dispersed, and in many neighborhoods, especially those of the upper middle class, there is minimal communality. In fact, one criterion of material success is to be able to go it on your own. Where I live, it might be weeks before I would know that a neighbor is ill, divorced, or even worse.

Today, though I am running late, it is not by much. If it were, I would go into the waiting room in order to explain my predicament to the patients. I would not send my secretary to do the dirty work. When I measure myself against the clock, I feel the tension increase.

As a student and later a resident, I had the naive conception that, after I finished my training, I could set my own schedule. In residency I had to adapt to the timetable of others and the duties they assigned. However, when I began my practice, free time did not materialize. As one might have predicted, I became a slave of myself and I continue both to fight this servitude and curiously to enjoy it. Primarily, professional aspirations drive me, but so do hobbies, such as collecting art and books, writing, and traveling. Also a large commitment, for which I have no apologies, is my family, and I enjoy being with them.

Although I yearn for time to contemplate, I know I would immediately use it up in some activity. I do have a dream, a vision from an experience many years ago when I was seventeen and on a student tour in Switzerland. I am lying in a flower-filled meadow on the outskirts of Interlaken on a sublime August day, hypnotized by the distant Jungfrau, feeling neither mind nor body, at one with the gentle ground below and the peerless canopy above. Will I ever again experience the pleasure of being anchorless without earthly chores, desires, or thoughts? Is it odd, even pathetic, that a professor at a prestigious medical school should want a few minutes that seem so rare to him and yet must be so common to others? Perhaps I am wrong; others may have the same lust for leisure.

How well I recall, and now better understand, the tired manufacturer who told me his supreme wish: to swap places for a weekend (note only a weekend) with one of his workers and play ball with his children, go to McDonald's—to shed his worries and responsibilities. And yet he recognized that each of his employees, when he drove by in his large car, envied him for the happiness they assumed he had. If Karl Marx were truly correct, all the upper middle class would be ecstatic.

So that is my burden: to carry within me, like a pacemaker, a little martinet, a homunculus technologicus who keeps me hopping to the twentieth-century tune.

I had a premonition of this type of professional life

when I was in my third year at medical school. It was an hour before the Yale game, and a patient shuffled into the medical clinic at the Massachusetts General Hospital. The senior resident said, "Here, take her. You will enjoy Miss Ames. She is extremely interesting." The word "interesting" sounded ominous, and it was. Miss Ames, seventy-five years old, was an annual visitor. She looked like the little old lady in the drug ads, even to having an umbrella, although the day was sunny. For Miss Ames, going for her annual checkup at the clinic was the high point of her year. Instead of being sorry that she was not seeing her previous doctor, she was glad because she had new ground to conquer. The senior resident, who also had a date for the Yale game, had already left, abandoning me in the now deserted clinic. True, there was a nurse at the other end, but she was having her lunch and was the epitome of disinterest.

"Miss Ames, how have you been in the past year?" I thought I was clever by asking her to describe only the past year so that I would not have to listen to her recounting what now filled four charts.

"Doctor, I have been fine, except for one thing."

She heightened the drama by not immediately revealing her problem but forcing me to ask what it was. She looked around to be sure that we were alone and then disclosed what she must have thought would shake a government: "My anus twitches." I knew then that I would miss most of the Yale game. A problem such as Miss Ames offered was not something to hear and dismiss casually. A complete gastrointestinal history was in order, a rectal examination, anoscopy—all this, and probably I would find nothing. Meanwhile, I did have to get the reluctant nurse, who groaned, "Not that complaint again." I had missed it, even though I had gone through the charts, heavy testament to the health of the patient and the thoroughness of the many doctors who had also taken their place across the desk from Miss Ames. Nevertheless, it would not be all bad, my being late for the game. At the cocktail parties afterward, I would have a good story to tell. But, of course, conscious of my importance as a physician-to-be, I would not use her real name.

"Everything is normal," I told her after I had completed my examination. "I do not know what is causing the twitching, but there is nothing unusual that I can find." Under ordinary circumstances, I would have discussed Miss Ames with the senior resident and the staff physician, but they were already cheering Harvard. By now Miss Ames has probably twitched her way into eternity but not into oblivion, since I remember her. I wonder whether she is in anyone else's memory. If so, it is certainly not in the way she remains in mine.

My work has no cadence. I push my way through the day in a jerky, unrhythmic fashion, with some patients requiring more from me emotionally than others.

Mrs. Mary Marinara, the next patient, is going to present me with a difficult decision that will take a lot of time and probably will result in an outcome she won't like. I have seen her before, but I advised her to return with her husband. She is twenty-eight, of average height, muscular and slim, with cropped black hair and dark skin, a devotee of yogurt and aerobics. Perhaps she thinks of sex as a calorie burner. Her dress is trendy: a tan, open sports jacket with a black handkerchief in the pocket to match a black vest with a yellow geometric design. She is wearing a brass chain necklace, black pants, and black shoes. Her open-necked blouse is like a man's shirt, with the cuffs sharply pressed. Two gold bracelets flank a gold watch with a black alligator band.

That I am able to describe her clothing represents an acquired skill, since sartorial particulars do not fascinate me. Nevertheless, I am aware of the style and effect of what a patient is wearing.

Like most doctors, I do not put details of dress into a patient's record unless, for example, the person was so unkempt that it might suggest a mental illness. In most instances, recording apparel is not essential to the patient's management.

We physicians, in fact, go to the extremes of not having our charts reflect a preoccupation with a patient's financial status, although we note it, since we have seen and talked with the patient and have exacted information about place of residence and type of occupation. We like to believe that we are treating the patient shorn of such externals as the type of clothing he or she might wear.

Physicians are very much aware that our office notes might be aired in court. A jury would not applaud a physician's Flaubert-like talent for describing an Yves Saint Laurent dress or a Gucci handbag.

Since Mrs. Marinara looks as if she is in the flush of fashion, one would expect her to act that way, with confidence and vivacity, but she doesn't. She speaks carefully and thoughtfully, not because she is profound but, I suspect, because she is under stress and does not want to make a mistake—another mistake. Although she says she wants larger breasts, I suspect she is complying to save a failing marriage.

At the time of her previous consultation, I dictated the following: "The patient states that she always wanted 'bigger breasts'; yet she admitted that only recently, after her summer vacation, did this become a preoccupation."

During that consultation, in response to my question about what her husband thought of the operation, she said, "He is like all men. He prefers girls with large breasts." Yet, in today's love market, her husband undoubtedly had known what he was getting. Small breasts did not impede his passion before; would it revive with bigger stimuli? For too many people, marriage is what Amiel called "the grave of physical love." That nineteenth-century bachelor and master of introspection thought this a "great blessing," because "it frees us from an obsession or carnal illusions and redeems one's freedom of mind." Judging from the results of most contemporary sex surveys, most respondents would not agree.

Mary Marinara's husband, John, is a good ad for his business, selling athletic equipment. In his early thirties, he is handsome, powerfully built, and well-dressed. He obviously goes to a hair stylist and has a Hollywood look, which makes him resemble a lot of other people.

Outside my office, his manner would be assured, but today he seems embarrassed, perhaps because he fears a situation that has gone beyond his control. He probably is afraid of exposing his feelings toward his wife. Most men whose wives want an augmentation will say, "This is her idea. As far as I am concerned, she is fine." They worry about the risk to their wives. Is this procedure dangerous? Does it cause cancer? Could she bleed or get an infection? Could she still nurse a baby?

Mr. Marinara asks none of these questions. He looks

unconcerned and detached; he has taken himself mentally out of my office, as he has from his marriage. I am witnessing the common crime of non-passion.

I explain to both of them that there is a 30 percent chance of having abnormal firmness and a distorted contour of the breasts as a result of scar tissue forming around the silicone gel implants. I show them the type of prosthesis that I plan to use; this I did previously with Mrs. Marinara. I am blunt. I have to be sure that she is the one who wants the operation and that she desires it for herself and not as an unconscious or conscious attempt to make, in my words, "things better between you two." She then looks down, and he says, "Whatever she wants to do is all right with me."

I know that she has already decided. She will have the operation to keep the marriage. She is willing to lie on a table, to take pain, and to risk her health—all this to preserve a family unit, which includes two young children. I pity her. I think of my daughters and feel sorry for them also. I hope they will be able to withstand pressures of our culture that make the woman the sacrificial lamb.

The Marinaras need family counseling, yet neither has admitted openly to having marital difficulties. It occurs to me that there is not much difference between the words "marital" and "martial." Maybe Nock was right: "Monogamy is the triumph of culture over nature."

For a few minutes, the Marinaras are united—against me—to prevent my penetrating their domain. I am the surgeon they wish to hire; that is my role—do your job, do it right, do not pry.

Right now Mrs. Marinara has an anguished pleading

look, as if to say, "Keep it simple, doctor. This is your specialty. We have the money. I am willing, and I am healthy. What more do you want? Please do it. Don't have me peddle myself from one office to another. It is demeaning enough just to go through it all with you."

I feel uncomfortable, and to give myself more time, I repeat again the mechanics of the operation: under local anesthesia with intravenous medication, two hours, outpatient, someone to take her home, pain medicine, no driving herself for a week, stitches removed in ten days. We are getting down to the line. I have decided that they are not going to like it. She who came asking politely will leave angrily. And I do not like anger, a weakness, perhaps, but I can't now change the way I am. I start to talk and listen to myself as if I am another person—that odd professional detachment, separating myself from them as John Marinara has done from his wife. I realize that what I say is put together well; it is not the first time I have done it. I feel apologetic for my glibness.

"As you know, I am a surgeon, and I make my living by doing it. In fact, with two daughters in school, it is to my financial advantage to operate as much as possible [we all smile and that will be the last time]. Yet, to be honest with you, I am uneasy about operating on you, Mrs. Marinara. Please excuse my frankness, but I have the feeling that you are embarking on this operation more to help your marriage than because you really want the augmentation [they both look uneasy]. In my experience with other patients, this rarely works. A family counselor will do more good than a plastic surgeon. At least I would hope that you would consent to see someone before having your breasts made larger."

I sit back and get the reply that I have heard too often: "But, doctor, my breasts have always bothered me. I really want this for myself, too." The word "too" reinforces the correctness of my analysis.

Mr. Marinara repeats that it is his wife's decision. He leans forward, impatient to leave.

"I guess we have reached an impasse," I say. I feel the satisfaction of practicing good medicine but also the remorse of perhaps being too rigid about somebody else's motivations. Am I being the "good doctor" like the "good boy"?

I am causing them pain, and I may be wrong in my judgment. Many of my colleagues would act simply on Mrs. Marinara's statement that she wants an augmentation, and they would schedule it. Perhaps her life would be better by their doing it than by my insisting on a psychotherapist's evaluation. I console myself by thinking that, if I have harmed them, it is better through omission than operation. Furthermore, I am not comfortable operating on her; that visceral feeling is my professional red light. My ego is not so massive that I delude myself by thinking that my surgical skills are so special that a patient will be at risk with anybody else.

Mrs. Marinara ends the consultation by getting up abruptly. "I guess there is no need for us to take up more of your time." We shake hands woodenly.

With another patient I did get involved in the unpleasant dynamics of a marriage. That experience made me wary of trying to solve marital problems through surgery. For some patients, plastic surgery can be a metaphor for something else, and the doctor can unknowingly participate in the wrong scenario.

Many years ago, a very tall young man, Aaron, a Harvard graduate student, consulted me because of what he called his "very large ugly nose." He was concerned also about his receding chin, which accentuated his parrot beak. As unattractive as he was, his wife was exquisite, the type who inspires envy in women and longing in men. She was also a graduate student, majoring in French. With her long blond hair, tanned, in tennis shorts (complete with racket), she made a painful contrast to her husband. She was not Jewish, as he was, and she had the best of her ethnic heritage, whereas, externally, he seemed to have the worst.

Throughout the consultation, Veronica, his wife, was very supportive. When Aaron mentioned that he thought his chin was "too small," she agreed, as did I. He decided that he would have a chin implant as well as a rhinoplasty.

He entered the hospital, had his operation, and recovered uneventfully. Because he planned to leave the hospital and go by auto the same day to New York City—his wife would actually drive—we decided to keep him in the hospital an extra day. But Aaron changed his mind since he felt he was doing so well. He wanted to get out sooner. No need to call his wife. She would be surprised to see him. She was, and so was the man in bed with her. I found all this out when a tearful Aaron returned to my office the following week.

He not only felt betrayed but, what is perhaps worse, foolish. He said that he had considered his surgery a way of bettering his marriage.

"Please understand. I still would have had the operation, but it might not have been now. I hate to admit it, but part of the reason that I went through all this was for her as well as for me."

In that situation, it is not uncommon for a patient to dislike the result of an operation, even when it has been done well and the anatomical outcome is excellent. I was particularly fearful because of the high dissatisfaction rate in males having had a rhinoplasty. However, Aaron did like his result.

He was not without humor, and at the time of his last visit said, "At least now I am a better-looking sad man."

The plastic surgeon, though concerned with appearance, has a responsibility to the patient to consider more than surface anatomy and emotion. Before doing an elective operation, he or she must take into account not just the person but, sometimes, the family. The surgeon's job is easier if those closest to the patient come along for the first consultation. Their interactions usually furnish sufficient evidence to know whether one will harm or help by operating.

Michele Gerbrick, whom I am now seeing for the first time, is a short girl with a bulbous, humped nose. She is with her mother—a tall, elegant woman, whose nose, however, looks unnaturally pinched at the tip, the sign of a previous rhinoplasty, I deduce. I am quite sure why Michele is in my office. I give Michele an information sheet to fill out. That her mother does it instead of Michele is a clue to their relationship. When I ask Michele why she has come to see me, Michele looks at her mother, who says that her daughter wants her nose changed. What her mother really means is that she wants Michele to have her nose changed. Michele, who is sixteen, and her mother radiate discord. The daughter is what the mother is not. Unlike her attractive, slim, and fashionably dressed mother, Michele is plain, stolid, and stocky. She seems to be saying, "I will not be like you, no matter how much you try." Her mother, undeterred, does the talking, while her daughter sits, head down, swinging her left foot back and forth. It is far from a heartwarming scene.

"What are your thoughts about having an operation on your nose?" I inquire.

"I don't know," she replies with a shrug.

The fact is that Michele would look better without the hump on her nose, and I do not wish to insert myself into a family situation that is ready to detonate. When I have to examine Michele, I lead her away from her mother into another room. I want to know her more and to be sure of her feelings about the procedure. Sometimes a child can want the operation but does not wish to admit it and will let the parents assume the onus. However, Michele, in response to my probing, is consistent in not acknowledging any desire for nasal surgery, though she has a deviated septum in addition to an external nasal deformity. She would need work on the septum as well as a change in the shape of her nose.

After we leave the examining room, I explain the procedure to Michele and to her mother. Michele would be in the hospital a couple of days; the operation would take about an hour and would be done under local anesthesia with intravenous supplement so that she would not feel much pain. I stressed to them that Michele would be swollen and black and blue and that she would have to wear a splint for about a week and have packs in her nose for a few days. Throughout this explanation, Michele remains sullen. I continue my explanation, even though I know that I will not operate on her, because she herself has expressed so little interest. I tell them that the final result after nasal surgery will be apparent only after six months or more. Since I would be changing the structure of the nose by removing cartilage and bone, the skin and soft tissue need sufficient time to shrink to their new contour.

Finally, there is no avoiding the central question.

"I am not sure how much Michele really wants this procedure. I do not think that she is enthusiastic about it. In fact, I detect more than a little resistance."

Michele looks at me differently now, even with a glint of pleasure in her eyes. Her mother becomes the protestant. She says, "Michele and I have discussed this many times before, and I think that we should go ahead with the operation."

"Michele, how do you feel about it?"

Michele does the wise thing. She says, "I would like time to think about it some more."

"I can certainly understand that," I say. "No one is rushing you, and you should take as long as you want in order to weigh the various things that we have talked about. Maybe also you would like to discuss this with your father."

Michele's mother looks at me in wonderment. Michele's father, I assume, is an obliterated human being, at least in his home. I am glad that I do not have to eat dinner with that family this evening.

Despite the mother's insistence that I schedule Michele, I resist. As they leave the office, it is Michele's mother who is pouting. I predict that I will never see or hear from them again. I also prophesy that Michele's mother will not give up, that she will find a willing surgeon, and Michele will capitulate. She may even like her nose; but a greater likelihood is that she may resent it, even if it is anatomically pleasing, because it will have been forced on her. The relationship between Michele and her mother will then deteriorate further. I feel I was best serving Michele's interests by bowing out.

In the case of Gloria Waldosky, the next patient, I will take a different route. Gloria, who is sixteen and has never met me before, is smiling nervously. She is short, slightly overweight, and is wearing a white and blue dress that looks too big for her. I understand her choice of clothes when I see from the record that she is in my office because of her large breasts. She is understandably reluctant to talk about why she has come and looks to her mother to supply the information. Mrs. Waldosky tells Gloria that "the doctor wants to hear it from you."

Gloria complains of pain in her back and neck, of difficulty in buying clothes since her breasts do not properly fit even into a 38 DD bra. She admits that she feels anxious when she goes on a date or to the beach. Gloria's mother, who also has large breasts, has encouraged her to seek what is called a reduction mammoplasty. However, Gloria's father is very much opposed to the operation. Although he has accompanied Gloria and her mother to this consultation, he has chosen to stay in the waiting room.

In my experience, it is not unusual for fathers and husbands to object to breast reduction. Most American males, from their adolescence, have craved buxom women. Many who have large-breasted wives are proud to squire them. They know that other men probably envy them and think that they must be "all man" to be able to have, hold, and satisfy such a woman—primitive yet prevalent thinking. Although one may protest that our culture is foolish in this regard, it does not change the reality of the tyranny of these attitudes, ridiculous or unfair though they may be. In fact, the obsession of males with the breast is part of the reason that Gloria is in my office. She resents that boys and men think of her in terms of her breasts and not as a person, a sentiment I have often heard from many older patients.

Gloria's past medical history and physical examination are not unusual except for her breasts, which are huge, extending well below her waist. In the words of another patient's mother, "She has breasts that just won't quit." Gloria's furrow marks from her bra straps are painful and deep. She is moderately round-shouldered, and her spine curves slightly forward.

I tell her that she has "too much of a good thing," and she agrees. I use the term "good thing" with her not just because of my male bias but because she has just mentioned a friend who had only one breast develop. Gloria's next question is almost predictable: Could I give her friend some of her breast tissue? The answer is no, because of immunologic incompatibility.

Mrs. Waldosky is in the examining room with us because Gloria wants her there. Gloria would prefer her mother being present rather than my secretary. As I examine Gloria's breasts, her mother looks away. I show Gloria and her mother where the incisions and scars will be.

After I examine her, I wish to photograph her. For this, she must stay undressed to below her waist. Gloria blushes, and I sympathize with her. I try to make it easier by saying, "I really know that you don't pose for pictures on Mondays, only Wednesdays." These photographs are an extremely important part of my record and influence my planning. They are as necessary to my work as an electrocardiogram would be to a cardiologist. Furthermore, photographs are also helpful in medical-legal situations. They are useful as well in reminding patients of what they looked like before operation.

After I take her pictures, her mother and I leave Gloria alone so she can dress. I ask Gloria whether she would mind having her father present for the next part of the consultation, and she says she would not. I realize I must convince him about the necessity of the operation. I will try to make him realize it is in his daughter's best interest for her to have a reduction mammoplasty. As a plastic surgeon, I do not like to be a salesman, especially with patients who wish aesthetic surgery. My usual position is that this is what you have; this is what I can do; you decide; I am available should you want me. In a patient with a malignancy, I would be much more active in my role. However, with Gloria, who is only sixteen, I feel strongly that I am more like her advocate because I believe that the operation will make her feel better about herself and will significantly improve the quality of her life now and in the future.

Mr. Waldosky is a huge man, whose clothes seem barely able to accommodate a bulging belly. He is polite but wary. I imagine that he could be extremely tough in his work as a contractor.

Gloria now returns to my office and takes a seat between her parents, as I describe what will happen to her should she have her breast reduction.

She will be in the hospital three or four days; the operation will last about four hours and will be done under general anesthesia with her asleep; there is a chance, although small, of infection or bleeding; there is likelihood of altered sensation in her nipples and areolae. Even though the sensations may be decreased, women who have had reduction mammoplasty tend to enjoy sex more because they feel more relaxed.

Because we have to remove breast tissue, we must cause scarring, and the probability of her nursing a baby will be less. To most girls of Gloria's age, the last point seems insignificant compared to their present difficulties of having to endure tremendous breasts.

I also tell the Waldoskys where the external scars will be, and I emphasize that they will be permanent. Although very bad scarring is unusual, it is still possible, since wound-healing is unpredictable. I also have to inform Gloria and her parents that with breasts as large as hers, there is also a chance of interfering with the blood supply to the nipple and areola. This might cause the nipple to die, a probability that is low, about 3 percent. Every surgeon doing this procedure and every patient having it must consider this likelihood. However, if the nipple were to lose its blood supply and necrose, it could be reconstructed months later.

Now the most difficult part of my recitation: mentioning the unlikely possibility of her dying. I preface this by saying, "I am going to talk about something that you might not ask me but that you might fear, as I probably would if I had to face an operation. Could you die from it? The answer, of course, is yes, but it would be an extremely rare event, probably less likely to occur than a serious accident if you drove from here to Chicago and back."

Gloria nods in such a way that I know this doomsday prospect was on her mind. Her parents look nervously at each other and then at Gloria, who surprises them by looking very calm, yet with her attention fixed on me and what I am saying.

I then repeat to her and her parents another truth: I have yet to have a patient tell me that she regretted having a reduction mammoplasty.

Mr. Waldosky, however, seems distraught, obviously unsettled by my litany of complications. He, I should mention, does not know his daughter's true breast size since he has not seen her undressed as a teenager. I do have a set of slides available for such situations, and I am able to produce another patient (whose face is not shown, but whose breast size approximates Gloria's). As I put these slides on the projector I use for this purpose, Gloria blushes, even though they are not her own photographs. Mr. Waldosky still does not believe the very large breasts either of his daughter or of the patient depicted should prompt anyone who is sane to seek an operation that is risky and potentially lethal. To Gloria's father, large breasts without scars are preferable to smaller breasts with scars.

But it is Gloria who eventually triumphs. "Daddy, please let me do it. You don't know what I have to go through every day. I hate these breasts." Tears come, and her father soon capitulates, like a giant struck down. In an about-face, the whole family now discusses when to schedule the operation. I feel elated, until I remember that Mr. Waldosky's initial misgivings have put so much pressure on everyone else that, unless Gloria's result is superior, we shall all be the recipients of his "I told you so's."

Being an optimistic surgeon, I count on the happy sequela, but suddenly I remember Mrs. Maria Figulla. I had to intervene also, but in a different family relationship. Thinking of her now makes me smile, but when I took care of her, I was not that happy. Mrs. Figulla was in her late sixties, a stocky woman whose square figure resembled a mailbox. She had been born in the ankle of Italy, as had her husband, whom she had met there.

Her breasts were gigantic to a degree that caused her much distress at night. Her husband, a carpenter, constructed a hammock on which she could place her breasts when she slept, in order to relieve the burden on her chest. Despite her obvious discomfort and what must have been a grotesque scene in the boudoir, and despite the opinions of her internist and an orthopedic surgeon, Mr. Figulla considered the operation an aberration and a hazardous indulgence on the part of his wife. With some trepidation, therefore, I proceeded, because his wife had told me that she no longer had the strength to fight against "my watermelons."

At operation, I took care not to leave her too small, but she still ended up a 38 C, a size that would have led other women to seek a breast reduction. No complications. Excellent healing. A delighted patient—for three weeks— then a tearful woman, sobbing in my office.

The problem: "My husband can't do it with me anymore." Mr. Figulla had become impotent. She quoted him: "I got a boy, not a wife."

It is easy to see the humor in this situation at a distance, but I confess I was very apprehensive. By what I thought was skillful surgery, I had ruined their marriage. I castigated myself, remembering Arthur Conan Doyle's remark: "There is nothing worse than an ambitious fool."

Guilt was not my only emotion; fear entered and dominated. What if Mr. Figulla, a powerful man, perhaps even paranoid, came after me?

It was obvious that Mr. Figulla needed a psychiatrist, and soon I began to think that I needed one also.

But how was I to get this couple to see a psychiatrist—an unlikely duo for the usual family therapist? Fortunately, the Figullas had a nephew who was a urologist, whom I called. He arranged an appointment for them to see a psychiatrist, and after he argued with them for most of a Sunday, they agreed to go. Amazingly, after just six visits, the miracle happened. Mr. Figulla was his old self and, I hope, cheerfully dismantled the hammock.

But one cannot live in the past with a patient in front of you. As the Waldoskys prepare to leave the office, I say to Gloria's father, "It's not easy being a parent." I mention that I have children, both daughters, who are twenty-three and twenty. We feel a collegiality of bewilderment. Being a parent confers an in-the-trenches experience. Others without children may write books about parenting, give lectures, and appear on TV, but they are gurus with even less substance than most.

chapter 8

Before I go to the hospital to operate, I have lunch: yogurt and a roll—the kind of repast that allows a dieter to eat the forbidden between meals.

As I leave the office, I scoop up the mail. Harold Nicolson criticized American diplomacy for having to leave the desk clean at night. For me, it is my survival.

The phone rings, but I am already down the corridor. I recall with amusement what an older doctor in my building did to avoid answering a call. So that his secretary could say that he was out of the office, he literally stepped into the corridor.

My schedule—seeing office patients Monday, Wednesday, and Friday mornings, and operating Monday and Wednesday afternoons and most of Thursday—has evolved over the years. At first, because most of my patients have elective surgery and could arrange their operations months ahead, I took the prized 8:00 A.M. time every day. Being first on the schedule freed me from contending with the delays of others. Surgeons in other fields rightfully objected, and the operating room adopted a "block" scheduling policy: it assigns a block of time to a particular service, which then subdivides it among its staff and residents.

The surgeon needs operating time as the hockey player needs ice. Access to the operating room is our lifeline. Usually plastic surgeons are not the most powerful politically in a university hospital or medical school. Although I am a professor of surgery at Harvard Medical School, I am infrequently asked to give classroom lectures to students. Any impact I may have on education is at the postgraduate stage.

We plastic surgeons are not usually the first group that an operating room committee remembers in assigning time. At the Beth Israel Hospital, we on the plastic service have nevertheless received extremely fair treatment. Of course, we ask for and could use more hours, but the complaint is like that of many husbands desiring more sex even if they would not avail themselves of it given the opportunity.

This sexual analogy is not outlandish. Most heterosexual male surgeons feel their masculinity affirmed by operating, as they do after having had sex. Both acts have a physical component. The word "surgeon" comes from the Greek word meaning to work with one's hands. And although Harvey Cushing, the first chief of surgery at the Peter Bent Brigham Hospital and the founder of modern neurosurgery, said that he would welcome the time when someone without hands could become chairman of a surgical department, he himself was a prodigious operator.

Cushing's remark was to emphasize the need for a surgeon who thinks well and broadly as a total doctor rather than as a proficient meat cutter.

On this sunny day and after the long morning, I have little enthusiasm for the operating room. I envy my secretaries who can remain behind. I had similar thoughts in medical school when I had to take an examination. I wished I could have been one of the men working on the grounds, cutting the grass. I sometimes wonder what it would be like to have the job of people who are unknown to me, whom I pass on the sidewalk. Although I have considered from time to time doing something other than plastic surgery, I do not know what it would be. I realize that I will never take that risk. I have to reconcile myself to the fact that by this age, fifty-five, I have already made a life statement that, despite my mild protests, will probably continue until the end. Sometimes, I think I will never outgrow my adolescent conflicts. Yet there is compensation; the momentary anguish makes me feel younger. I rationalize that perhaps sustaining these inner battles is my way of combating aging.

What would it take, I ask myself, for me not to go to the operating room on this beautiful day? I know myself well enough to realize that my guilt would destroy any leisure I could have obtained furtively. From the pressures of my profession, I have had the curious inversion of thinking of time as belonging to someone else rather than to me. During the day, a free hour seems like sixty minutes taken from a patient, either in the office or in the operating room.

I get into my car to drive the usual way to the hospital. I pass the Hebrew College, where one evening I participated in a panel on the ethical question of whether a physician should participate in planning for mass survival from a nuclear war. The government was then asking certain hospitals to set aside twenty-five to fifty beds in the event of a thermonuclear blowup. As a member of Physicians for Social Responsibility, I tried to show the futility of such preparations. Nuclear conflict would cause such immense destruction that it would render impossible any effective medical aid. Furthermore, and this was the crux of the argument, by such efforts as designating hospital beds in case of nuclear war, we physicians would be indirectly implementing a nuclear holocaust by perpetuating the illusion that a thermal nuclear war is survivable.

I remember that I had urged my hospital not to comply with the Department of Defense's request for bed allotment, but I later found out that the hospital had already acquiesced without discussion or debate among the staff. That a Jewish hospital, albeit technically nonsectarian, should take this action, almost secretly as far as I was concerned, upset me, especially since we Jews pride ourselves on our ethical concerns. Moreover, the Beth Israel Hospital, which has always been sensitive to moral issues, was a regular sponsor of these symposia on medical ethics. Yet it had followed the establishment line; whereas the establishment hospitals, Massachusetts General and the Brigham and Women's, had rejected it. Jewish insecurity again, perhaps.

Just before I turn into the Beth Israel's grounds, a car passes me. Its bumper sticker reads: "In tennis, love means nothing." And, I muse, what does it mean in love?

Interesting how people use the rear end of their cars to assert their individuality, to make themselves heard.

Those who do not know whom to hug should drive around town for suggestions. If we believed the stickers, we would attain sexual nirvana from embracing garbage men, nurses, bears, and chemists. I imagine the quizzical looks of archaeologists if these printed injunctions were to survive; they might be our Dead Sea Scrolls. For that matter, what about possible future digs unearthing breast prostheses in the coffins of females?

I park my car in the garage and once again enter the hospital lobby. I pass an internist, to whom I say "Hello," but he ignores me. As someone said of Horace Greeley, this doctor is a "self-made man who worships his creator."

This minimal exchange with a supposed colleague increases my awareness of whom in the hospital, and under what circumstances, I acknowledge with a greeting, a smile, a nod, or a handshake—or all of the above. In general, people of the same sex and rank respond to each other most quickly with the greatest enthusiasm. The pecking order, of which most in a hospital are aware, dictates that those high in rank should be the first to offer a sign of recognition. A chief of service, for example, could hail a resident from twenty yards away; but a resident who greeted his chief first at such a distance would seem forward and his behavior inappropriate. Not to be reciprocated in kind or better disturbs me. No matter what our age, we feel vulnerable to rejection.

The Beth Israel Hospital, with approximately 475 beds and 2,200 medical and nursing personnel, is so large that not even a memory stunt man could recall everyone's name and position. There is a large full-time and part-time staff. In general, those in a full-time capacity derive some of their salary through the hospital or medical school; whereas we part-timers earn our income totally through private practice.

I am one of the few part-timers in charge of a division at any of the Harvard Medical School hospitals. Although part-timers may outnumber the full-timers, the power is with the latter. Throughout the country and certainly at Harvard, the part-timer is historically on the way to extinction, despite statements to the contrary from hospital chiefs and trustees. I deplore the situation, and I startled the Harvard Medical Alumni when, at my twenty-fifth reunion, I gave a talk titled "Once Upon a Time ... There Was No Part-Time." I said in part:

He [meaning me] remembers happier days before the Great Schism, when there was less cliquism in the care of the sick, when there was no part-time or full-time, when no one wore an armband. Then he was younger, of course, and perhaps naive; but he thought that the battle was against disease and suffering. Now he sees diverting conflict between those who should be allies. The cynicism of having lived a half-century leads him to wonder how there could ever be peace in the world, among vastly disparate nations, if those of the same country, even of the same state, and those of similar values, education, and professional milieu seem unable to bridge without rancor a comparatively small gap.... This alumnus regrets the change that has led to subdividing the genus physician into the species part-time or full-time.

In medical school and residency, he recalls, those who taught him clinically were judged by the standard of their patient care.... Should we remember and reread William Osler in a different fashion because his annual earnings were large even by today's standards? ... They who bear the brand of "part-time" resent its connotations. Implied is a partial commitment, an incomplete dedication.

How can I be part-time? one wonders. Do I not rise early in the morning, work in the office and at the hospital helping patients, teaching residents and medical students, and then return home in the late evening, at least five to six days a week? Except for vacations, am I not always on call? Do I not plan to stay in one location for the rest of my professional life? To whom am I part-time? Certainly not to my patients, not really to my hospital, and not in performance and devotion to my medical school, even though it may regard me as such.

I remember how I felt at the conclusion of my talk. I had the pleasure of knowing what I said was true. There was silence for a few long seconds, then loud applause. I felt sadness more than exhilaration, because I realized that my remarks, though well-crafted and attentively heard, would never change anything. I was both a sociologist and the aborigine he describes, soon to be pushed out of his village by a new highway.

My consternation was not just fear of becoming a forgotten clinician, a common fate for men more remarkable than I. Most medical students, for example, would find it difficult to identify Lister, the founder of modern surgical aseptic technique, or Osler, the paragon of the humane and broad-visioned physician. I was unhappy because of what I perceived to be a lack of genuine appreciation for what medicine is all about: a patient who is ill and a doctor who may be helpful. To portray the medical school as an uncaring monolith would be inaccurate. It cares probably as much or more than most similar institutions. To refer to the Medical School as "it" is a convenient oversimplification of a sprawling realm of seventeen affiliated hospitals and medical centers, all their personnel, a faculty of more than 3,000, a student body of about 700, and the hundreds of thousands of patients, without whom no medical school would exist. Though Harvard is large to me, it is small relative to our society, a dwarf in the world. Economics largely determines its existence and direction. Money may be the root of all evil, but without it the walls of Harvard Medical School and its hospitals would crumble. Heads of clinical departments are now immersed in fiscal matters to a degree unimagined when they chose an academic career. To maintain their potency and reputation, they must provide care, engage in teaching, and do research, all of which require dollars. Academic medicine, whatever else it may be, has become a retail business. Attracting patients is now not just a preoccupation of part-timers. Full-timers are being sent by their chiefs to open offices even in shopping malls for availability and visibility. This competition between part-timers and full-timers for patients has led some university hospitals to close their staff to part-timers or to tax their earnings.

Most physicians, myself included, have an ambivalence about the medical school and hospital in which we work, much the same way as we might have about a parent who protects and rewards but also punishes. We want the hospital and medical school to shield us, but we also want independence. We accuse a hospital of being too restrictive and intrusive, comments that we as teenagers made to our parents, and now as parents we hear them from our children.

For many physicians whose parents have died and whose family ties are weak or absent, the medical school and the hospital become the family structure. Even minor events assume a magnitude, absurd and unjustified. What seems so important to me in the midst of a working week becomes minuscule on the weekend.

I have been a visiting professor at many medical centers and hospitals. While they may differ in their tradition and physical structure, they are the same in one major respect: human beings run them. Ultimately, the type of treatment a patient receives depends upon the character and competence of the individual physician. A hospital's reputation may attract patients, but that alone cannot cure them.

I am once again in the lobby of the Beth Israel Hospital. I notice an abundance of plaques commemorating the generosity of donors. While all hospitals have their share of these public acknowledgments, Jewish hospitals seem to have more. But, in fact, who notices these plaques? Who stops to read them? Who remembers the names, or if they do, who associates them with a particular individual or family? To be sure, the older staff may make the connection, but not so the younger attendings or the residents. The idea of being remembered is tantalizing to a prospective donor. Usually it is a futile hope, however, since one cannot easily purchase immortality unless he is a Croesus or a Caesar. Who escapes from what Amiel called the "pit of oblivion and the humus of history" is indeed capricious, even unfair. That the millions of Jews murdered by Nazi Germany will in centuries be nameless while Hitler will be immortal seems unjust and absurd. I anticipate the obvious rejoinder: Better to be forgotten and to have done good than to be remembered for having done evil.

I am conscious of the decision I am now making either to take the elevator or walk to the third floor. Usually the elevator wins, the last luxury before five or six hours of work. My rationalization is that I used the exercising bike a half-hour this morning—a routine that would be a chore if I were not able to read at the same time.

I "push" the button, not an accurate description. I strike the button after a zigzag approach with my index finger, the arm rigidly extended, an enactment of a fencing maneuver that I learned when I began the sport in my first year at prep school. What surfaces during a day still surprises me.

I ask myself whether my life is so empty or whether I am so bizarre that I am actually making a decision about a couple of flights of stairs. Will I ever be able to do away with these petty considerations? Maybe even Einstein on his deathbed thought of buying a different kind of pencil.

As I leave the elevator, someone says, "He must be a surgeon." However, since I usually carry a large black bag that a patient made for me, I sometimes am taken for a pharmaceutical salesman. Once, someone who saw me go into my office and then come out asked, "How did you ever get in to see him?"

Most people have an image of what a doctor is supposed to look like and how he is supposed to behave. They have learned this from previous visits to doctors or from reading about medical events or from seeing such transactions on television. I remember a delightful instance that shows how well trained the public is in proper medical behavior. At the Peter Bent Brigham Hospital several years ago, a distinguished-looking man entered the operating room suite and told the head nurse he was from a university in the West. He asked to see an operation. With formality, he was ushered in and watched attentively. The surgeon, in fact, asked him how he would do the procedure, and he said, "Much the same way as you, but I think I would extend the dissection." The surgeon replied, "As a matter of fact, I was thinking the same thing," and proceeded to do it. A few days later, we found out that the visitor had been making the rounds of the various Harvard hospitals with credentials of his own invention. Nevertheless, I had no doubt that he would have been magnificent at the bedside, and if he had opened an office, he would have been popular immediately. He had a serious, thoughtful manner and an ability to make everyone think that he had been there before—the type that every headwaiter instinctively directs to the best table.

I pass through the door of the operating room with its forbidding sign: AUTHORIZED PERSONNEL ONLY. I greet the nurses at the operating room desk and those in the holding area, where patients wait before their procedure. I think of those who work in the operating room as my friends. Indeed, I spend more time with them than with many I invite to family celebrations. Because we are together for so long, our relationship seems deeper than it is. But physical proximity is not the same as friendship among peers. In an institution like a hospital, equality is sparse, the legal kind easier to achieve than the social.

Those of us who work in the operating room are always surprised when we meet each other outside the hospital. The usual comment is the cliché "What are you doing here?" It is as if we are saying we have no validity anywhere else than in the OR.

Today, I see Jerome Waters, a general surgeon in his fifties. He is not in operating room garb but in a suit and he is scrutinizing the schedule for today. If he should die tomorrow, that is the image he will leave with me. Unlike most of us who look at the list of operations in order to locate our room and to estimate the starting time of our case, his purpose is to see what other surgeons are doing. A subterranean thinker, he is competitive and unsure of himself to the point of begrudging a colleague another person's gallbladder. He fits the Russian proverb: "The dogs bark at the man who rides fast."

I am thankful that my motor responds to a different switch. Perhaps it is that as a child I received copious love and security from parents who taught me not to "waste my energies" on what others thought or did, but rather to realize my potential, whatever that might be. My mother used to say, "There is only one original, but there are many copies."

Miss Brewster is lying in bed with her eyes closed, the curtains drawn on the sides but not in the front, so that the nurses can observe her. Her intravenous of 5 percent dextrose and water is running slowly. The premedication seems effective.

"Hello, sleepyhead," I say, then realized that I used a diminutive expression, something a father would probably say to a daughter. Does anyone else notice this? Probably, since the female nurses are sensitive to patronizing males. Perhaps my remark will not register with Miss Brewster, who is drowsy. I rationalize that even if she thinks I am treating her like a child, perhaps she will find it comforting, not degrading, in these few minutes before her operation.

"Oh, doctor, I must have been dozing."

"Well, if one of us has to be asleep, it's better that it is you."

I secretly envy her nap. That I could be so irrational as

to covet anyone's preoperative status, especially one who has had cancer, disturbs me but reflects my fatigue, which I attribute to having just eaten lunch, albeit a small one. I would not like to admit to myself that my weariness is due to my getting up early and working hard. I know, however, that once I begin to operate, my fatigue will vanish.

I tell Miss Brewster that I must change into my scrub suit and soon will join her in the operating room. I go to the dressing room, which is up a flight of stairs, to my locker, the small space of which I have utilized maximally. In it, I have not only a toilet kit but also a cassette player, tapes, breast prostheses of many shapes and sizes, a magnifying lens, operating room shoes, towels, and an extra scrub suit should none be available. I select a large size and recall unpleasantly that I used to wear a small or medium when I was a resident. The color is pink, especially chosen to stand out, to prevent those in the operating room from leaving and returning from the relatively dirty environment of the rest of the hospital.

The chief resident, Mat, joins me, and we discuss today's case. He is already a skilled surgeon, in his final months of training. He comes from Hawaii, where he plans to return to private practice. Modest and competent, soft-spoken yet determined, he is almost an anachronism in this slick world of the self-proclaimers. Perhaps his character is due to his close family upbringing in the Japanese-Hawaiian tradition and to the values that his parents have transmitted to him.

I greet the nurses who will be with me this afternoon. Their first names I know better than their last. The turnover in staff has been more than we surgeons like and more than the hospital wants. Those who work in the operating room do not have it easy; they have long hours and are usually tired because this area of the hospital is understaffed. Many have gone to other jobs in unionized hospitals that will pay them more. Operating room personnel feel isolated from, and forgotten by, the rest of the hospital. They like being left alone, but they complain from time to time of being neglected. When the heads of nursing come for what is billed as a "frank discussion" with the operating room nurses and orderlies, these administrators appear ill-at-ease, like visitors, not nursing colleagues.

What the operating room staff think about their work conditions concerns me. They put in the same hours there, even more than I do, but earn far less. They would like their jobs much more if they earned more—not surprising or unreasonable. Productivity would increase along with their wages if they shared the income. The time between cases would dramatically shorten if they received a percentage of the day's take. Whenever a policy like this has been adopted, it has had success. In the sea of capitalism, American hospitals are enormous islands of socialism battling inundation from rising costs.

To have nurses share in the profits is almost unthinkable in a Harvard hospital, but it is a reality elsewhere, in some of the ambulatory surgical facilities in the United States.

The relationship between operating room personnel and surgeons is intriguing and, to my thinking, has been insufficiently studied by psychologists and sociologists.

How surgeons and nurses interact varies with the culture. I recall visiting a plastic surgeon in Paris at his private clinic. I was told to change in a room where I found two nurses in their bras and panties. I excused myself, thinking that I was in the wrong place, but they said that I was not. I changed, blushing like an adolescent, not of today but of my generation. When I arrived in the operating room itself, my change-mates were there, but the surgeon never introduced them to me; nor, for that matter, did I ever meet his assistant, a surgeon. The hierarchy was inviolate: being half-naked together was not synonymous with professional familiarity. Americans may forget this; Europeans never do.

I now enter my operating room, carrying my ever-present black bag as well as my cassette player and tapes. I ask Miss Brewster whether she would like to hear music. She is surprised that I can provide it. Her preference is classical. She chooses Mozart from an array of old masters. I play the tape softly in order not to disturb the anesthetist now hovering around her. The anesthetist will soon apply the mask to her face, but it will not be done until I arrive. In this hospital, no one is put to sleep without the surgeon in charge being there.

"Louise," I use her first name now, "we are all ready, and everything is going along beautifully. When you wake up, you'll have some pain but we'll give you something for it. I'll be there when you come out of anesthesia."

I purposely avoid the phrase "regain consciousness," since I want her to think of her anesthesia experience as falling asleep. I don't want to stir up what she and most patients fear: being unconscious and unprotected, not in control, with one's life in the hands of relative strangers, though skilled, people one has met just hours before.

This fear is not ludicrous. A surgical error, in fact,

would be less hazardous to her survival than an anesthetic mistake. I am glad for the extraordinarily competent department of anesthesia at my hospital. This makes my own level of anxiety low when I operate. I am aware and vigilant but not nervous.

Louise Brewster is now breathing through the mask; the anesthesia bag inflates and deflates rhythmically. She is receiving nitrous oxide and oxygen, and a few milliliters of Pentothal are about to go into her vein.

"Miss Brewster," the anesthetist is saying, "you will soon get very sleepy. Before going off, you'll probably have a garlic taste. That's due to the Pentothal that I am about to give you."

She smiles and a few seconds later says, "I do taste the garlic."

"Compliments of Julia Child," I say.

She tries to smile but then breathes heavily. Quickly the anesthetist opens her mouth, inserts the lighted laryngoscope, and passes a tube down her throat, through the vocal cords into the trachea. He tests the position of the tube by placing the stethoscope on her chest and making certain that her breath sounds are good and equal on both sides of the chest. A grave mistake would have been to have passed the tube without realizing into the esophagus rather than the trachea or to have pushed it too far into the trachea and to have obstructed her bronchus. A patient could then die because of lack of oxygen and poor aeration.

With tape, the anesthetist fixes the endotracheal tube to Louise's lips and chin. We call an orderly into the room to turn her onto her right side, in order to operate on her back and left chest. During this time, I check her carefully, making certain she is receiving oxygen as well as halo-thane. Many years ago, during my residency, one of my mentors used to say, "I don't care what else they give a patient, so long as they give oxygen."

In turning Miss Brewster, we take every precaution not to dislodge her airway—her lifeline—or to cause pressure on any bony prominence. An unconscious patient who must lie still for a few hours is very susceptible to skin breakdown. Although this does not happen often, it does occur with enough frequency to make us very careful not only for the patient's sake but for ours because of medi-cal-legal liability.

The nurse places cushions around the ankles, between the knees, and under the right hip. A small blanket roll goes under her right upper chest and armpit to facilitate expansion of her lungs. The anesthetist is assisting her respiration. A machine is automatically filling and empty-ing her lungs about eight times a minute. So that she will not fight against the rhythm of the machine, she has re-ceived curare, which has paralyzed her own respiratory excursions.

Throughout this period of turning, the anesthetist care-fully checks her pulse, blood pressure, and temperature. She is "hooked up," as we say, not only to an electrocar-diogram but to an electronic temperature monitor. In ad-dition, to decrease the likelihood of thrombophlebitis and pulmonary embolism, she has alternating-pressure pneu-matic tourniquets on her lower legs. These will remain until tomorrow morning when she will be able to walk. The circulating nurse places on Miss Brewster's thigh the grounding plate for the electrocautery, which both coagu-lates vessels and cuts tissue, depending upon the preference of the surgeon. This machine is called the Bovie, the name of the inventor, who with the great neurosurgeon Harvey Cushing made this technique reliable and easy to use.

Now a nurse pulls down Miss Brewster's covers and removes her hospital gown. Her genital area is not exposed, something that I was also trained as a resident to avoid doing. In those days at the Brigham, if a patient, either male or female, were needlessly or cavalierly uncovered, the senior nurses would censure us. Even today, clear and valid was the message: the patient, even when unconscious, has an intrinsic dignity that deserves our respect.

Looking at Miss Brewster, I wonder why few artists have painted a partially nude patient in an operating room. There are surgeons and anesthetists who are competent painters and could do this. Yet I suppose that even a public so jaded as ours would find macabre and improper (an odd word considering today's mores) the depiction of someone naked and helpless in a setting that is medical and presumably confidential. The average viewer would empathize with the patient and would consider the artist's work a betrayal. Quite different are the paintings that people have long admired, such as the old doctor sitting thoughtfully, sadly, helplessly, at the bedside of a dying child.

Although we have come to accept as beautiful, or at least tolerable, the depicted nude body, most of us would find revolting a canvas portraying a procedure being done to a patient, such as a pelvic examination or a sigmoidoscopy. Even the devotees of photorealism would not be enthusiastic purchasers of such pictures, showing the patient in discomfort, demeaned in the process of being helped. How curious it is that the public, which has been able to assimilate the cruelties of concentration camp art, has been spared the supposed blessings of modern medicine.

Miss Brewster, still partially uncovered, reminds me of having done an abdominoplasty (misleadingly called a "tummy tuck" to make it seem like a simple, no-risk operation—which it is not) on a celebrated woman to whose nether region many famous men had already paid costly homage and many more would happily have done so. True, she was beautiful and her conversation and intellect were above average. Yet, when I saw her unclothed, I had difficulty comprehending why she and her Jade Gate were worth all that trouble and turmoil. Several families had foundered as their patriarchs became embroiled in her loins. Like George Kaufman's supposed remark to a friend about seeing his play at a disadvantage—with the curtain up—my viewing the patient nude places her at a disadvantage, since her curtain is down.

A surgeon in an operating room is not entitled to too many wide-ranging thoughts. There is, after all, a living body to be dealt with. For the patient, surgery is no allegory. Whatever the act of operating may be for the surgeon, the consequences for the patient are irrevocable; they are ominous in their irreversibility. The patient asks only "Was it successful or not?" not whether it was meaningful to the surgeon or whether the surgeon felt like a medical knight or knave.

After making sure that Miss Brewster is in the proper position, I go to scrub. The circulating nurse is now putting on sterile rubber gloves to wash the patient's chest and back. She will use an iodine preparation called Betadine. Several times during her hospitalization, Miss Brewster has been asked whether she has allergies. Occasionally, a patient does have a hypersensitivity to iodine, and we would then use something else. I instruct the circulating nurse specifically where to wash the patient. The nurse in charge of the instruments, called the scrub nurse, has already put on her gown and gloves and is arranging our tools for the operation.

All these measures to enhance sterility we accept as routine, without reflecting that each step along the way to aseptic technique was arduous. Pasteur, Semmelweis, Lister—all had to fight the attitudes and dogma of inflexible men intractably opposed to the germ theory of infection. Masks and rubber gloves are standard now, but even I can remember about thirty years ago visiting a New England hospital where a surgeon took off his gloves to get a "true feel" of the tissues and refused to cover his nose with a mask. These bacteria will not dare to interfere with me and my work, he seemed to say.

As I am scrubbing my hands and arms, I remember that as a medical student taking an introductory course in surgery, using dogs, we had to apply lampblack to our hands and forearms. Then, blindfolded, we had to scrub off the material as vigorously as possible for a period of ten minutes. We understood the point of the lesson when we saw finally how unmethodical we had been about scrubbing, leaving large areas, especially between the digits, unscrubbed.

Today, I scrub about seven minutes. Being a surgeon, I am somewhat impatient, but I consciously tell myself, "You may be in a hurry, but the patient deserves the best. Don't cut corners on her time, with her life." Finally, my hands feel clean. I realize this is ridiculous to say, because we cannot perceive bacteria, but at least there is a familiar sensation of hands thoroughly soaped and scrubbed.

With my arms raised at the elbow in order to avoid contamination by dropping them below my waist, I enter the operating room, pushing open the door with my knee. I relish this moment. It is like what I imagine entering the corrida must be for a matador. No fatigue now. I feel alive, tingling, youthful. Perhaps I even look that way, since my face and head are covered. True, there is gray hair at the sides and back of my head, and my eyes have put in more than a half-century of looking—seeing more than observing. I remember what an old surgeon once said to me: "It's a shame we have to swap youth for experience." Strange that I should be thinking of myself when everyone else in the room probably assumes I am thinking only of the patient.

I gown and glove and apply another iodine solution to the patient's back and chest. I lay on the sterile towels and sheets, a satisfying ritual that makes me feel like an acolyte.

The intern is opposite me; everyone is in position. I look at the anesthetist, who nods. With Mozart in the background and the patient on the table, the scene has romance and majesty, ingredients I like. A good surgeon in the operating room is at least half-actor. He or she needs to be, I believe, to lead the group. Any leader must be. Of course, the surgeon should be more than an actor, but a diffident and unsure surgeon will have a difficult time in the operating room, and so will his patient. He also will have no fun, nor will the others.

I like the tradition of the operating room, its order, rites, details, and its hierarchy, with myself in the primary role, at least on this side of what we call the ether screen—a three-sided piece of metal attached to the table over which we place the drapes. The anesthetist in this way has complete access to the patient's head but is still out of the operative field and will not transgress the sterile barriers.

In the operating room, I feel like a surgeon; in my office, I often think I am a physician, even occasionally a psychiatrist; but here there is no ambiguity. I am egotistical, I suppose, because I like the responsibility of being a surgeon, the chance and challenge of making a helpful difference in somebody's life and the concentric lives of those close to that person. I enjoy what I do because I can see the results of my work soon, sometimes by the end of the operation.

It seems as if this day began thirty-six hours ago. There may be weariness in the background but not boredom. When I was much younger, I worried about using myself up. Is that so unusual a fear for a Jewish boy with an attentive mother? Now when I am tired, I do not become anxious, only irritable.

My thoughts wander to Europe and center on those upper-class Englishmen I used to meet when I traveled who were geniuses at leisure, not only during the summer but perennially. But I also think: what advantage is it to be rested when you die?

Now my mind, like a super Concorde, has recrossed the Atlantic, and I am back to reality, to Louise Brewster, whose flesh I now cut. There is almost a shock to the tissues, which do not bleed for a second or two. Then comes the expected ooze—good color, signifying good oxygenization of the patient's blood. Layer by layer, I guide the knife to the desired plane. The human body still causes me to marvel. Wondrous also is how our society has evolved so that it cares about the health of its members, at least on occasion, and it provides people like me with complicated facilities to help someone else.

The press of the operation does not prevent me from thinking of the irony of our culture, expending all this effort to aid one life, not even to save it, and yet doing comparatively little to reduce the chances for war, which would cost us all this—my eyes sweep the operating room—and would extinguish two billion human lives, plants, insects . . .

My manual duties end this brooding.

I watch myself cutting through the tissue. Being able to dissect in the correct plane is something that younger surgeons find difficult. It is a question not only of seeing but feeling with knife or scissors. Being in the right plane means less bleeding and less danger for the patient and also less work for me. Now the cautery. I think about Bovie again. For a dollar, he sold his patent to this electrocautery in exchange for ensuring that his name would forever be on the machine. He died in poverty but still lives, as a noun (the Bovie) and also as a verb, since we surgeons say "Bovie it" or "It was Bovied." Somehow I feel close to Bovie, because I once wrote an article on his life and think that somehow, if I grant Bovie immortality, perhaps there is a chance for me.

I continue to cut and coagulate. The operation goes faster and the blood loss is less with the electrocautery.

Halsted, who pioneered modern surgery, stated, "The only weapon with which the unconscious patient can immediately retaliate upon the incompetent surgeon is hemorrhage."

The objective of this part of the procedure is to isolate a four-by-eight-inch oval piece of skin connected to the underlying muscle (latissimus dorsi), which I intend to dissect so that it is attached at one end only by a small pedicle containing the strategic nutrient artery and vein. We must take every precaution not to injure these vessels since they are the blood supply to this flap of muscle and skin.

After an hour and a half, this large muscle with its central piece of skin lies free. The color of the flap looks excellent—pink, indicating that the blood supply is good.

I then make an incision through the old mastectomy scar in Miss Brewster's chest, where her breast used to be. By separating the tissues under her armpit and on her chest, I create a tunnel through which I introduce the muscle-skin flap from the back, rotating it frontward, where it now lies, an amorphous clump of tissue that soon will become her new breast.

The resident and I now begin to close the gaping wound of her back. There is pleasure for me in working closely with someone younger, skilled, and dedicated, who represents the continuity of my specialty.

I realize that plastic surgery has become a minor religion that, though lacking a God, has nevertheless exacted from me more than eighty hours a week of work over the past twenty-five years. I have performed with fervor and, I admit, fatigue from time to time. How easy it is—too easy—for the professional orbit to spiral outward, obliterating so much else in its course.

The needle holder carrying the stitch, called "chromic

gut" and made from sheep intestine—it used to be called "catgut"—passes upward through the dermis of the skin on one side and down through the skin at the same level on the opposite side. Each time, as we tie the ends, the large hole in Miss Brewster's back becomes smaller. Repairing the damage we had to inflict in order to get skin and muscle for the breast is the hallmark of a plastic surgeon's trade. Our motto should be "stealing from Peter to pay Paul." Since the closure of this wound is, as we surgeons say, "routine," it becomes more of a pleasure than a task. In fact, sometimes I find myself suturing in time with the rhythm of the music. Strauss waltzes provide a better tempo, but Mozart will do.

Isolating the vascular pedicle of the flap was more demanding than this part of the operation. Now, we can indulge in extraneous conversation; all nonsurgical. Everyone participates: anesthetists, nurses, surgeons, resident. Although some surgeons prohibit talking and music in the operating room, I do not. In fact, I consider both a necessity. Working with as little emotional tautness as possible is good for everyone's health. But more than that, I enjoy knowing more about the lives of those around me.

When the circulating nurse, Noreen, talks about her two boys and her husband and their new home, I am interested.

The scrub nurse, Liz, amuses us with her account of her last date, a "real weirdo." We laugh, and that by itself is worth five milligrams of Valium. The conversation is not all one way. I am not always the listener. In fact, like many surgeons, I divulge in these surroundings things that would probably embarrass my wife: family skirmishes, personal complaints about life as a husband, a father.

Many surgeons use the arena of the operating room to tell jokes to women that they would never relate anyplace else, except perhaps in a locker room. I do not know whether this is symbolic intercourse with women who, if one is married, are presumably unavailable. Without sounding like the model child in a Sunday school class, I never enjoy hearing or telling such stories because I think it is a sign of the raconteur's sexual frustration. As yet, I have never heard a female surgeon in the operating room tell similar jokes. Only rarely does a female nurse reciprocate with humor in kind. The male residents and technicians usually refrain from these carnal capers. Everyone seems to defer to the old bull.

The discussion now is about marriage. As I look around the operating room, I think about nurses and their marriages. Some nurses I have known in the past have married men who, to their thinking and mine, were not their match in intelligence, sensitivity, and ambition. One nurse told me frankly that working with doctors all day, even having to endure their arrogance, created a letdown at night. The males with whom she then interacted were a disappointing contrast, being less educated, doing less important work, and having less socioeconomically.

On the other hand, some nurses are very happy not being married to a doctor since that role is not an easy one. Many books have been written about the "doctor's wife," and now there will no doubt be many about the "doctor's husband." Most doctors give to so many others that it is difficult for them to give much to those near them. The quality of what should be their closest interpersonal relationships is often poor. Perhaps we doctors are overwhelmed by the prospect of a relationship that has parity, since it necessitates give and take. Furthermore, one cannot control a love relationship the way one can attempt to control interaction with patients and fellow workers, particularly those lower in the hierarchy.

We are putting in some of the skin stitches, made of nylon, and are getting ready to place the drain, a flat silicone tube with perforations that will later be attached to suction in order to take away the blood and serum that will accumulate in the wound over the next few days.

As a surgeon with a sense of history, I am mindful of how Louise Brewster and I have benefited from medical progress. Aside from aseptic technique, she has had the blessings of anesthesia, new safe drugs, sterile intravenous solutions, and a better understanding of physiology and metabolism. Even the sutures and drain represent technological advances. In the past, less than a hundred years ago, some surgeons were using unsterilized horse hairs for sewing skin together. As a consequence, many patients developed tetanus.

We now prepare to turn Louise on her back, with the same precautions that we used in turning her for the first time. Still sterile, I support the flap, which is now in its new location on the chest, while others help rotate the patient. They then change their gowns and gloves, as do I. The circulating nurse, gloved, washes the patient's chest with iodine antiseptic solution and the resident repeats the process.

While I am scrubbing my hands again, I observe the patient through the window above the sink. It is important always to be aware of the patient, not to forsake him or her. By the time I reenter the room, the team has the patient redraped.

I now do a little more dissection so that the tissue from

the back will fit easily into its new location. I fold the skin and muscle into the pocket I have made. Our plastic surgical jargon would have us say, "the pocket I have created," but it seems too prepossessing. Anything to do with "create" is best left in Genesis.

As the new breast takes shape, there is a rustle of approval among the team. The women in the room identify with Louise and voice their pleasure at the appearance of the reconstruction.

I stitch the muscle-skin flap to the surrounding tissue in such a way that it projects, to simulate the opposite breast, although in truth the match will be only approximate, not perfect.

I place another drain into the patient's chest anteriorly and close the wound in layers as we did in the back. The patient is now ready for the dressings, and we sit her up with the aid of the operating room team. We wrap her chest in bandages but loosely, in order not to interfere with the flap's blood supply and her respiration. By this time, Miss Brewster has regained her ability to breathe, and the anesthetist now removes the tube from her trachea.

I think to myself: "Three hours of my time. A tangible result. I am glad I am in this specialty."

My obituary will identify me as a plastic surgeon, a career I never anticipated when I was in medical school. In fact, the first time I scrubbed in an operation, I contaminated myself three times, each incident requiring a change of gloves and gown. The memory of the exasperated surgeon and nurses glaring at me causes me discomfort still. I could barely endure the ordeal that mercifully terminated after two hours.

That night, when I telephoned my parents, I told them

---

of my dismal day. I vowed never to return to the operating room, at least voluntarily. My father advised me strongly to reconsider, to try again. "Never quit when you're behind," he said.

Now thirty-three years later, the operating room has become my second home. People consider me a surgeon, and I am used to being one. I feel experienced in my role but not so old in it that I cannot empathize with the frightened novitiate who enters this specialized environment.

Plastic surgery and my work are part of our society's hypertrophied system of gratification. It is as if some master urban planner realized that unless we keep people busy wanting something and providing something, the masses would wander about without purpose. In a culture that has in its large cities more than one drugstore, bank, and ice cream parlor on every block, the presence of a superspecialist, like myself, is understandable. It seems to be imperative that each of us create as many needs, even more, than we can satisfy.

The idea of becoming a person who could do something others could not occurred to me when I was ten years old. My father and I visited a wool-waste factory that belonged to a neighbor, a kindly, elegant man who had fled Germany because of the Nazis and soon became a successful manufacturer in this country.

Taking a small sample of cloth from a pile, he challenged my father and me to tear it in half. Despite our strenuous efforts, neither of us could. He then did it easily and said to me, "Remember, in life, it is more important to know how to do something than simply to use strength." That axiom characterizes plastic surgical technique.

chapter 9

At this stage professionally, I do not do much pediatric surgery such as cleft lip and palate repair or craniofacial operations. I refer those patients to surgeons for whom these problems are their major interest.

Plastic surgery now has so many subspecialties it is impossible for anyone to do everything equally well. Fortunate is the patient whose doctor does not consider himself omniscient and remembers that the patient's body belongs to the patient. Most are grateful for a helpful referral and regard it as an act of honesty in a world that has come to expect the opposite from many physicians and surgeons.

Every patient unknowingly will meet one of three types of surgeons. The first is the young surgeon who, in the flush of having just completed his residency, needs little stimulus to operate. The saying is, "A virgin surgeon needs no urgin'." He believes that his scope is unlimited, even if his experience is not. Compared to the older surgeon, he can do a greater variety of procedures, many of which have developed within the past few years, long since the older surgeon left his residency. The fact that someone younger can do more does not necessarily mean that the patient will get the best treatment. The range may be greater, but the depth less. Oliver Wendell Holmes said that the younger doctor knows the rules, but the older doctor knows the exceptions. In surgery, there is another requirement: there must be the match of the right operation to the right patient. The younger surgeon, because initially he usually lacks many patients, will spend considerable time with each. Patients are convinced they have found a doctor who unites competence and concern, and that may indeed be true.

But the young surgeon frequently has high financial commitments. He may have a new office, a wife, children, and a new home. Many young doctors have pledged too much of themselves to the bank. During the course of their college and medical school and residency training, they have accrued enormous debts. Even if the spouse works, the added income may be insufficient for a number of years to repay their loans and to finance an escalated life-style. If the young plastic surgeon has also decided that he or she needs an operating room facility in order to attract aesthetic patients, there is a further financial strain, and the threshold to operate lowers. The decision to "do a patient," as we surgeons say, should depend upon the individual's medical needs and not the doctor's monetary requirements. Patients who are impressed by a large, opulent office may not realize that, when they called to schedule an appointment, they almost ensured themselves of an operation by someone with wallet hands.

The surgeon in the second stage of his or her career has been in practice fifteen to twenty-five years. Now "successful," with many referrals from physicians and patients, he or she is likely pleased with the fruits of a growing reputation, gained usually through competence. More recently, however, since advertising is now legal, clientele may come from the efforts of the media more than from those of the surgeon. Hiring a public relations firm and using advertising are other expenses that soon become formidable.

The older surgeon, to accommodate the large influx of patients, may cut corners. There are several ways of doing this, and all of them are bad. The first is to spend less time with each patient, being less punctilious in obtaining a history and doing a physical examination. Sometimes the doctor assigns history-taking to the patient in the form of a questionnaire or has the office staff assume that function. The doctor may have all the material in his possession but may not evaluate it or assimilate it properly. Mistakes, minor at first, in patient care soon happen, but the surgeon's ego is so enormous that it obscures his lapses.

The patients, in fact, may not realize that they are getting less for their money from a doctor, because they are proud of having someone whom others consider famous. Some even prefer a plastic surgeon who is more technician than physician. They fear the scrutiny and probing of a careful doctor, who might find something serious. These patients want to control their body and their destiny; they want their plastic surgical transaction to be superficial, with less medical-surgical connotation, and consequently, they hope naively, with less physical danger.

The more discerning patient may complain that the

doctor in demand did not spend enough time. The surgeon is now in the elaborative phase of his profession: more patients, more secretaries, more nurses, more operations, more gadgetry, including inevitably a computer. The surgeon soon falls into a pattern that could be fatal for a patient and disastrous for himself—taking on more people and projects than he can handle with excellence. But with the large number of patients, he may not notice those who are dissatisfied. The volume dilutes them and deludes him. The surgeon may continue to believe that his or her performance is better than it truly is.

If referrals from other surgeons or from operating room nurses or residents decrease, the surgeon should be wary, since these people probably know his work better than anyone else. Yet what may cloud his vision are the Very Important People who come. Management or mismanagement of the rich and famous is too well known to document here. Some surgeons get great pleasure as their egos swell in proximity to patients who possess power. The surgeon may cater to their whims instead of adhering to the standards of good medicine. The paradox is that what produced the surgeon's good reputation were most likely hard, careful work and reverence for detail. That is why the VIP has come to him. Yet the surgeon, flattered by having such a patient, may bend like a pretzel to avoid what the patient might consider "inconvenience." Thinking more of the patient's social status than his medical problem happens more frequently than many patients realize.

A hospital trustee recently relished telling me that he was able to wrest an "early" appointment with a doctor on his staff. In actuality, by exerting his influence, he was risking his health, since that particular doctor left Hippocrates for hype years ago. Now he relies on the residents, as we say, "to bail him out."

The middle years of a surgical life offer the surgeon, whether he or she knows it, the choice of having skills dwindle or develop. In a competitive, changing profession, there is no such thing as staying the same. The unsuspecting surgeon may be enjoying the scenery while effortlessly treading water, but suddenly the undertow will suck him under.

Doing yesterday's surgery well today is insufficient. Because financial success will continue, at least for a while, with that type of performance, the surgeon may not be cognizant that he or she is out of step. Though I like Thoreau, I do not believe that the surgeon will find consolation in the Walden dweller's saying: "If a man does not keep pace with his companions, perhaps it is because he hears a different drummer."

Every surgeon from time to time must ask himself or herself a few hard questions. Am I performing as well or better than I once did? Am I advancing with my field? Should I be doing or learning something new? Am I capable of doing it well?

Every human being is too precious to fall victim to the pride or ignorance of a poorly qualified surgeon. Before embarking on a new procedure, it may be necessary to spend time with another surgeon to learn a better technique, to attend symposia and meetings, and to read medical publications with an eye to adopting some of the more recent methods in order to get improved results. The middle stage, therefore, requires a different kind of exertion, which the younger surgeon may fail to realize or appreciate.

In this middle phase, the surgeon runs the risk also of

endangering his or her personal life. Marriages flounder as the surgeon, usually male, succumbs to the attractions of patients, nurses, colleagues, students, or secretaries with whom he spends more time than he does with his family. Perhaps female surgeons will soon duplicate this unrewarding behavior.

Many surgeons cannot manage success, often more difficult to surmount than failure, which may have united husband and wife in a common goal. With high achievement, each may go his or her way. The fast-lane doctor may soon become dependent upon other stimuli to keep going: alcohol and other drugs are a refuge from more patients, greater responsibilities, and further commitments.

Being in this middle stage myself, I see the dangers, and I do admit that sometimes I take on more than I should, but I try to modulate my overreaching, at least from time to time. Fortunately, I have a wife whose judgment and sense of proportion are excellent. I try to listen to her and to my children, who also let me know when I am stretching myself too far. Frequent vacations, especially my regular month-long August hiatus, have kept me somewhat within bounds of moderation.

Nevertheless, I do see the tendency in myself, as someone said of Balzac, of having to go alternately to the extremes in order to stay in the center. A surgeon, or anyone else without a perception of the middle ground, may soon fall victim to the numbers game. He or she may gauge success by quantity rather than quality, by the number of procedures and the amount of income. I have long realized that for myself each day should be something more. I wish I could say that every day of my life has been a piece of art that I can sign with satisfaction. Would that it were!

Nevertheless, I try to do a few things well rather than doing too many things, some of which turn out only mediocre or worse.

Dupuytren, the famous French surgeon of the early nineteenth century, said, "Nothing is to be feared so much as mediocrity." But mediocrity can occur in the pursuit of excellence. At a university hospital, for example, the very busy surgeon trying to meet an impossible schedule of teaching, practice, research, and administration may let the resident do more and more without adequate supervision. Not surprisingly, the patient has not been informed. The surgeon may leave the operating room before the case is finished or may arrive after it has started. He or she may wander in and out for coffee or to make phone calls. In the hospital where I operate, this is not so, but I have observed it elsewhere.

In plastic surgery, the surgeon is usually present throughout the entire operation because we prefer to apply our own dressings. The dressing may be a critical factor in the operation's success. I am compulsive enough not only to apply the dressing but also to remain until the anesthetist has removed the tube from the patient's trachea and I can accompany the patient to the recovery room.

I say this not to applaud myself for adhering to what is really basic surgical deportment but to emphasize that success in surgery as in other fields depends upon details. While it is true that our society functions by having a distribution of responsibility as well as of authority, some work the system to the detriment of other persons. In medicine, there may be no second chance for the patient—there is no "Play it again, Sam."

The doctor in the middle phase of his career frequently

has another characteristic, an unflattering one. When he was younger, an older surgeon probably told him that where he wanted to practice was already overcrowded, a standard remark from someone who wishes to preserve his or her economic leverage. The younger surgeon, now older and well-established, may also tell someone junior that there is no room for him or her, when in fact there is. At best, the older surgeon usually reacts ambivalently to a new arrival. He wants the spotlight for himself, even though he may inwardly acknowledge that he cannot do everything. Someone younger with fresh skills may make him face the unpleasant reality that he is getting older and that his skills are waning. After all, medicine does progress.

The middle-phase surgeon grudgingly accommodates someone younger in the hope that the younger surgeon will take emergencies that he is happy to shed. In plastic surgery, for example, the younger surgeon usually pays his rent through emergencies, but as he becomes established in his practice, elective operations soon crowd the schedule. If he has to spend the night doing an emergency, he will be fatigued the next day for his regular list of procedures. With time, relief may replace alarm on the part of the older surgeon because somebody else is coming to share the bother of night call.

Finally, if health holds, the surgeon enters the third stage of his professional career. Like the old bull, or old cow, he or she may try to assert potency by coupling, but with the wrong patient. If he does not accept the fact that he must confine himself to those areas in which he still excels, he will soon have an inordinate number of complications. He will be an example of the "raised eyebrow" syndrome: the eyes go up in the operating room when nurses, residents, and anesthetists realize that old Dr. X should not be doing this one.

Is the answer a fixed retirement at sixty-five or seventy or seventy-five? Perhaps, but many times the younger plastic surgeon should be the one to terminate his or her career because of numerous bad judgments. That individual, however, is fortunate to be judged not by his actual performance but by his future growth. In that respect, the older surgeons are more indulgent than those who are younger. The justification is that with time, someone younger should get better but someone older will certainly get worse. My father quotes a saying: "The only trouble with growing old is that there is no future in it." As I mentioned, my father practiced psychiatry at eighty-three, but it is a rare surgeon who could do his work at that age without harming patients. Manual dexterity and physical stamina are necessary for surgery, and those are not the strengths of the later years.

I operated upon Jamie Hebert for a cleft lip when I was in Stage I of my career; I am seeing her now in Stage II; and I hope to see her and her child in the final, lift-off phase.

Some older surgeons are the last of the slaveholders. They may employ someone younger to do the operating. They may have a succession of these assistant doctors who will remain on salary long enough to accumulate patients and sufficient money to enable them to leave the older doctor in order to establish their own practices. Expropriating the efforts of others is, of course, a basic tenet of capitalism, corporate life, and academia. As editor of a plastic surgical journal, I receive many articles that have been obviously written by younger surgeons who have done the research; yet the name of the older surgeon will be tacked on at the end, or even, outrageously, at the beginning. The *droit de seigneur* is something that should cease but probably will not. I have always made a point of taking myself off a publication unless I have truly contributed to it. I would rather be thanked in the acknowledgments than misrepresented in the authorship. Many older surgeons do the opposite, to demonstrate to colleagues as well as to themselves that they are still a force to be reckoned with. Yet, when some people's names appear on a laboratory study, everyone knows that they would be as unlikely to do research as to picnic in Albania.

I accompany Miss Brewster to the recovery room, where I greet her as she emerges from her anesthesia. I am not sure that at first she knows who I am, but she smiles and squeezes my fingers. I call her father and speak also to her mother, who joins us on the phone. I then call her male friend, as I had promised I would.

My message to all of them is the same: the operation went very well, no surprises, no problems. I hope the rest of her recovery will be as uneventful.

They thank me for letting them know and ask me the same question: would it be "possible" or "advisable" for them to see Louise this evening?

I tell them she will be in the recovery room for a couple of hours before returning to her own room. They can see her there. Although she will be sufficiently awake to converse, she will be tired and in pain. It would be a good idea to keep the visit short.

Miss Brewster's male friend says that he will not visit her this evening but "later" in the week. I deduce that he would prefer not arriving at the same time as her parents.

I drink some orange juice, which every surgeon's lounge seems to have. It is a dependable friend to replenish the surgeon. I then dictate the operative note while the procedure is fresh in my mind. That account should contain information about the nature of the procedure, the names of the surgeon and assistants, the type of anesthesia, the indications for the operation, the findings, what was done with a clear statement of surgical objectives and whether they were achieved. For Miss Louise Brewster, I think that they were.

In the operative note, I mention also the estimated blood loss (less than half a unit) and the fact that the sponge count was reported as correct (no sponge inadvertently left in the wound). Although the operative note is important, I find it tedious to relive the case, and that is why no television program ever shows a doctor engaged in this chore.

I think once again about Louise and calculate that in four or five days she will be going home, if she does not have a fever. We will be removing her drains prior to her discharge.

I physically leave the surgeon's lounge, mentally separate from Louise Brewster, and go downstairs to the holding area, where my second patient, Mrs. Jean Cummings, is waiting for her operation. To be able to switch in this fashion from one patient to another is important. It usually is not difficult, unless the first operation has not gone well. It is hard for a surgeon to get up his courage and enthusiasm when he or she has just experienced a defeat. In much the same way, it must be difficult for a baseball player to come to bat after having struck out a couple of innings before.

I plan to remove the extra skin from Mrs. Cummings's

upper and lower lids. She is fifty years old, and this operation is a birthday present from her husband, an engineer. Jean, as she wants me to call her, is ostensibly a happy, uncomplicated woman, a housewife and mother of four. She is moderately overweight and once told me, "I know I should lose some pounds. But I had a lot of fun when I put these on."

She impresses me as the kind of woman who has never had hard deliveries or incapacitating back pain. To satisfy my curiosity on these points, I inquired. Without modesty, I confess that I was right. I doubt that she, like another patient having a similar operation, will ask me for a note to her husband "to get out of sex for three months."

Jean is active in the affairs of the school her nine-year-old daughter attends. I am sure she not only volunteers to help out at parent-teacher get-togethers but also stays for the cleanup. She is devoted to her own family but also to a legion of aunts, uncles, nephews, nieces, and cousins. I imagine that there is always enough food in the house for anyone who drops in, and I am sure that many do.

Jean's knowledge of art, literature, and classical music is minimal. She is not an intellectual, does not pretend to be, and does not regret it. As far as I can determine, she has never participated in a political-social cause such as an antinuclear demonstration. But she would be the first to cook dinner and carry it over to a sick neighbor. So many people I know in academia love humanity in the abstract but somehow cannot bring themselves to do anything generous for a particular person outside their own immediate family. It is much easier to sign a petition or a check than to give of oneself and one's time.

Jean has a whole-face smile. She is not one to hold back.

She does not seem apprehensive now, probably because she has wanted this procedure for some time.

"My shades are closing," she said at the time of her initial consultation, referring to her upper lids. "And I don't like these suitcases." She pointed to her baggy lower lids.

"I was always after my mother to do something about her eyes but she never wanted to."

"Why not?" I asked.

"I guess because she came from a different generation," Jean replied.

The anesthesia for Jean's operation will be local (lidocaine with epinephrine, which acts to constrict blood vessels and reduce bleeding). She will receive also Valium and morphine in small doses through an intravenous line that the resident has already started in the back of her left hand.

"Let's go, doctor," Jean says cheerfully.

We bring her down the corridor into the operating room, where a tape of Barbra Streisand is playing. I had the feeling that she would like that, and she does.

I help transfer her from the litter to the operating room table, which I crank up so she is in a semi-sitting position. This gives me a more accurate idea of what her eyelids will be after operation. I will have less likelihood of removing too much skin, causing a permanent pull-down of her lower lids—the basset hound look.

I give her a small amount of Valium and morphine intravenously. The Valium irritates the vein, and she complains of the "stinging." Soon, however, she says, "Wow, I feel sleepy. Not a bad feeling, doc. I think I'll come back every week."

The nurses tuck her right hand by her side and keep the

left arm outstretched at ninety degrees for easy access to the intravenous.

I leave the operating room, scrub, and return to dry my hands and put on my gown and gloves. I wash off her face with an antiseptic solution, hexachlorophene. I then dry her face and ring it with sterile towels and sheets. I use a blue marking pencil to plot the incisions. She gets more Valium just a minute before I insert a small needle into her skin to inject the local anesthesia. She gasps and groans, a reminder of how similar the sounds of pain are to those of pleasure. Am I perverse for thinking this? I put the anesthetic into all four lids. I wait seven minutes for the local anesthetic with epinephrine to take effect.

I approach the upper lids first, removing skin as well as a small strip of muscle. I coagulate the bleeders with a small battery-powered cautery (not the large Bovie, because I do not want the possibility of a spark injury to the eyes) and push on the upper lids to expose the bulging fat.

Jean, who is usually talkative, is silent throughout the procedure. I tell her from time to time that all is going well, and she smiles.

I remove the fat from two areas of each upper lid and then close the skin with a running-stitch 6-0 nylon, a small suture that looks like human hair.

For the lower lids, I make a tiny incision beyond the eyes laterally and with sharp scissors cut parallel to the lower lids but high under the lashes, which I am careful to preserve. I turn back a flap of skin and muscle to reach the protruding fat in three areas of the lower lid. At this point a nurse who has just finished a case in the other room comes in, because she says that she eventually wants to have this procedure and would like to see how I do it. I grasp the fat with a hemostat and the pressure causes Jean momentary pain. I cut away the fat with scissors and cauterize its base.

I drape back the skin and muscle and ask the patient to open her eyes and gaze upward. This maneuver also helps prevent taking away too much skin. I want to remove enough to get an improvement but not enough to get a complication. I excise a small amount of extra tissue, and then I approximate the skin edges with interrupted stitches of the same type of nylon I used for the upper lids.

I now ask Jean to look at my hand to count the number of fingers I hold up, to be certain that her vision is normal. Blindness is a very rare complication of an eyelid-plasty, and in fact, when it happens it is usually later, several hours after the operation. Yet, for the sake of good medical-legal protection, I want to know the present status of her eyesight. She sees perfectly well, as expected. I put into each eye a bland lubricant and gently apply dressings soaked in ice water to reduce the swelling, the black and blue, and the pain. I do not push on her eyes for fear of harming them. The cold dressings rest gently on her eyes.

Throughout the procedure, she has had only minimal pain. As we lift her onto the litter, she thanks us all. We turn up the head of the bed so that her face and eyes will have less venous pressure and presumably less swelling and pain. I accompany her to the holding area, write orders, and make out a prescription for Demerol, which she will fill at her own pharmacy. She will go downstairs where her husband is waiting and where she will remain for another hour; then she will go home.

I have already given her a detailed sheet of instructions. The important thing for her is not to exert herself, to get into bed, to keep her head elevated, and to continue to apply dressings for the next twelve to eighteen hours. She will be able to go to the bathroom. I tell her to call the office in the morning, not only to make an appointment for stitch removal in five days, but also to let me know how she is doing. She thanks me again, and I thank her for being a good patient. I do not mean this as a patronizing gesture, but when somebody is uncooperative, it is difficult to do my work and to give the patient an optimal result. Yet it is the surgeon who must assume the responsibility of enlisting the patient's aid in his or her own operation, if it is done under local anesthesia.

If the patient is still recalcitrant in spite of heavy intravenous medication, then I obviously have made a mistake in scheduling that person for local anesthesia on an ambulatory basis. Under these unpleasant circumstances, it is better to terminate the procedure and have the patient return on another occasion. The worse course is for the surgeon to give a hazardous amount of intravenous medicine, then to plow ahead, becoming angry at the patient and his team and eventually achieving an inferior result. As I have told the residents on many occasions, it is very difficult for us surgeons to stop our unfinished work—we dread surgicus interruptus.

Before I go to dictate my operative note, I call Mrs. Cummings's husband, who is waiting below. I want him to know that the operation went well, and I again go over the postoperative instructions and offer to answer any questions that he may have.

At the end, he says, "She's quite a girl, isn't she?"

I agree, of course, and think how pleasant it is to hear a spouse voice admiration for his mate. Although some women might object to his calling her "a girl," I would bet they have an excellent relationship.

I then dictate my operative note into the telephone. On the receiver, there is a playback button, and it is always reassuring to hear one's voice. It is terribly frustrating for me to have a dictated operative note lost. The too familiar words of those in the record room are a minor agony: "Somehow, it never came through, doctor. We'll check it again. Drop back in a couple of days."

That's a sure sign that one will have to redictate the operative note.

My next patient, Mrs. Rose Dember, forty-two years old, has arrived in the holding area. She is here for a nipple and areola reconstruction after having a mastectomy on her left side three years ago. She has suffered what she calls "H and D—humiliation and degradation," referring to her deformity.

Because of the spread of cancer to her lymph nodes under her arm, she has had irradiation as well as chemotherapy. Mrs. Dember is divorced and works as a secretary to a radiologist. Her children are both under the age of ten. Being a single parent, she has justifiable concerns about their future. She knows that her prognosis is "guarded," an unpropitious word, almost trite, that is distressingly close to "hopeless."

A year ago, I rebuilt Rose's breast using a silicone gel implant placed under the pectoral muscle of her chest. The breast has remained soft and has satisfactory symmetry with the other breast.

Unlike Mrs. Dember, many women who have had

breast reconstruction do not choose to have the nipple and areola made. One of my patients thought this reflected the poor self-esteem of women in general, afraid to ask for what was really theirs. That same patient also said, "After all, a breast is not a breast until it has a nipple."

The operation for building Rose Dember's nipple and areola uses the tissue already on the chest wall in the area of the breast to make the nipple, and a skin graft from her upper thigh to fashion the areola.

The color match with her other nipple and areola will not be exact since the upper thigh skin is lighter. But tatooing or sun tanning will usually minimize this discrepancy.

We shall do the nipple-areola reconstruction with a little intravenous supplement of Valium and morphine as we did with Mrs. Cummings. Mrs. Dember does not want to be asleep. The idea of having this operation on an outpatient basis pleases her because, like most women who have had cancer, she feels she has already spent too much time in hospitals.

For Rose, we must get two areas of her body ready for surgery: her chest and her right groin. Since I want to compare both breasts, the nurse will have to wash off her entire chest. This means she has to lie with her upper body uncovered. In addition, I need to have her inner thigh exposed. I sympathize with her having to be conscious in an unpleasant, unfamiliar setting that is also frightening, surrounded by masked male surgeons, her right leg turned outward, her groin and genital area in view. I try as best I can to cover her with towels.

I also say, "Rose, you're plucky to endure all this.

Thank heavens you spent your summers in a nudist colony, and you are prepared for it."

She laughs at what must seem like a preposterous statement. Yet I know from her eyes that she appreciates my understanding how embarrassing and demeaning this is. Sometimes, patients will say after I acknowledge what I think must be their distress, "That's all right. I have no modesty left."

Sometimes I believe them, but other times I think it is a cover-up—literally.

Many patients are willing to disrobe freely when their breasts have first been reconstructed, but in a few weeks they are more modest. This is a good sign that they have adopted my breast as their own. Adding the nipple and areola later confers considerable credibility.

Mrs. Dember has another problem to face, being cold. The operating room is kept slightly cooler because we who work in it become overheated underneath our gowns and the strong operating room lights. As the nurse washes Rose, she feels cold, and I do not make matters better when I repeat the iodine scrub.

However, as I place towels and sheets around her, she feels warmer. We are ready to begin—I forgot something, the music. I tell her what tapes we have, and she chooses Pavarotti, resisting The Grateful Dead, which Amy, my scrub nurse in her early twenties, would like to hear and not so subtly tries to get Rose to choose.

With the patient awake, we must be careful of what we say. Many years ago, I was removing, under local anesthesia, two skin cancers from the face of a movie producer. He had been in town for the opening of a film. The unsuspecting nurse announced to us both that she had just seen "the world's worst movie." You guessed it—his! I tried to kick her foot gently to signal her to stop.

"Dr. Goldwyn, are you trying to play footsy with me?"

The poor producer said nothing, but his bleeding increased, and the nurse taking his vital signs recorded a rise in his blood pressure. It seems more comical now than it did then.

Each door to this operating room now has a sign that says "Patient Awake," so nobody entering will make an inappropriate comment. Remarks such as "Oops" or "It's bleeding" or expletives are bad indiscretions. Residents understand they should not argue with me during the case should they feel they would have performed the operation differently. I would be happy to later discuss the matter in a more neutral setting. Most residents are sufficiently skilled so they can indicate with a nod, oblique language, or a finger any asymmetry, for example, they detect. I am grateful for these suggestions, as I am for those that might come from nurses. The surgeon who is so authoritarian that he squelches helpful comments ultimately harms the patient as well as himself.

Like baseball players, surgeons do physical things in view of onlookers. There are some surgeons who love to show their manual dexterity. They may exhibit more flourish in their hand movements than is necessary or prudent.

One of my colleagues once made fun of such surgeons by saying, when I was watching him operate, "You will notice that at no time do my fingers ever leave my hands."

Because Mrs. Dember has reduced sensation in the area of the breast, she feels only slight pain with the injection of the local anesthetic. I incise a circle with a diameter I have already calculated to approximate that of the opposite areola. In the center of the circle, I cut another circle which will be the nipple. I shall project it by making a deeper cut, with care not to interrupt the blood supply to this central core. The nurses also like this procedure because they can see the nipple actually being born. I stitch the edge of the central plug of tissue onto itself at its base to get the desired projection.

My other patient was right. Mrs. Dember's breast is getting to look like a breast now that a nipple crowns it.

Now I have to reconstruct the areola. This will require a skin graft to cover the raw area I produced by using the tissue folded on itself for the nipple.

Since Rose has normal sensation in her inner thigh, she will feel pain. I ask the nurse to give her some intravenous Valium just before I make my injection. The circulating nurse then moves the light so that it is where I will be working.

I have to wait five or six minutes for the local anesthetic to do its job. In my impatience with this necessary delay, I remember my Uncle Harris, the lawyer, telling me about a client who said to him: "Don't rush. It doesn't take me long to wait a half-hour."

I recall also how Dr. Gustave Aufricht, the pioneering nasal surgeon, used to pass this interval by sitting on a large chair that his nurse produced at just the right time. With sterile towels in his hands and eyes closed, he sat immobile. After the seven and a half minutes (never more, never less), his scrub nurse tapped an instrument and he got up to begin the operation. I am not that cool, and I move from side to side of the table, arranging and rearranging the instruments that have already been perfectly arranged. Finally, with a needle, I test the area of her thigh to be sure that she is numb. She is, and I take an elliptical graft of full-thickness skin and have the nurse wrap it in a saline sponge to set aside.

Every plastic surgeon can recall an excruciating episode in his or her life when some hapless nurse threw a graft away by error. Even if it has been tossed in a bucket, it usually can be retrieved, then washed in antibiotic solution, and used. Though most surgeons would not publish these incidents for fear of malpractice litigation, their anecdotes confirm the fact that infection seldom results and the graft usually succeeds or fails as if it had never been put through that trial.

Nevertheless, I watch very carefully where Donna, the nurse, places the graft. It is late in the day, and since we are all tired, mistakes are more likely now.

I close the donor site of the graft with chromic for the deeper layers and nylon for the skin. I take the graft and make a small hole in it at center through which I put the new nipple; the graft then becomes the doughnut, the new areola. I use silk stitches to anchor the graft and then later place wet cotton to form a dressing, over which I tie the silk, causing pressure on the underlying graft, thereby enhancing its take, since bleeding will be less and immobilization better.

Now we put some four-by-four-inch dry dressings over the left breast and a small dressing on the groin and hold them in place with paper tape.

"I'm glad it's over," Rose says, smiling. "But actually I thought it would be worse."

I stress to her that she must not change the dressing on her breast or even take off her bra until she sees me in the office next week. She also should not shower, since the dressings must stay dry. She can replace the small dressing on her groin.

I give her some dressings and tape for that purpose and a prescription for Demerol, since she will go home in an hour or so. Ordinarily, I would keep a patient like Rose overnight, but she wants to go home because she doesn't want to worry her small children.

Rose's parents are waiting for her downstairs. She lives with them, and because she works, the grandparents are also parents again—not like the old days of fewer divorces when parents with married daughters could look forward to being just grandparents. Now her elderly mother and father may have to raise her children by themselves if Rose loses her fight with cancer.

Another patient who endured a mastectomy but whose prognosis is excellent told me that "cancer makes an ordinary person into someone extraordinary if she survives." She also observed that, when a woman reconstructs her breasts, she is also reconstructing her head, her life. Rose, because of the spread of her cancer, is unlikely to fare as well as that other patient.

Although I get great satisfaction in doing breast reconstruction after mastectomy, it is rare that one finds anything humorous in this situation. However, with Mrs. Edna Forbush, a sixty-year-old widow, there was a comical incident.

A year previously I had reconstructed her left breast with an implant and three months later built her a nipple and areola.

Mrs. Forbush was an extremely religious woman, a born again evangelist. On numerous occasions, she had told me that "God had directed her to me." At the time of her last visit, she was standing half-dressed with an enormous cross hanging between her own breast and the one I had made. She told me she was extremely happy with the result. She came toward me and put her arms around me and held me, looking into my eyes.

"Make this wonderful experience complete for me. Become a Christian."

I replied, "I have enough trouble being a Jew."

I then had the peculiar thought that here was a white missionary, half-dressed, trying to convert someone who was fully dressed—the reversal of the usual situation.

The orderly has arrived to take Rose downstairs. I look at her, and she gives me a thumb's up sign. This brave gesture stuns me inwardly because I know what may soon happen to her. Nevertheless, I smile broadly and look as confident as she tries to be.

Like a rat returning to its cage, I go to a booth to dictate my operative note and then return to greet my last patient of the afternoon, Sara Whiting, a twenty-one-year-old black aspiring model. She wants her nose less negroid. After much deliberation and a few visits with me, she has decided to let me narrow her nasal bones, decrease the flare of her nostrils, and build up the dorsum of her nose, the part that most people would call the top.

When Miss Whiting discussed her surgical plans with her family, there was considerable opposition. In fact, her older brother, active in civil rights, accused her of running away from being black. Her father and mother were disappointed in her because they also felt that she was abandoning her heritage, in particular the family nose.

Sara countered by pointing out that her brother preferred black girls with light skin. She showed her parents a number of magazines that cater to blacks, to demonstrate that many of the models were not "typically black."

Sara and I discussed whether she truly wanted the procedure and understood the anatomic consequences. We both agreed that males, mostly white, dominated the modeling business, and they decided what blacks should look like. Her situation reminded me of another saying of my Uncle Harris about supermarkets that sold oranges sprayed to make them look orange. "Shouldn't an orange know what color it should be?"

Sara's chief support has been her boyfriend, Harold, a musician whom her family does not like. They interpret his approval of Sara's action as a way of sharing her income, which presumably would be higher if she got the modeling job she wants. Although Sara welcomes Harold's emotional backup, she is independent and determined. Sara's family objects to Harold's occupation because, in her words, "They say that 'any black man could do the same thing,'" meaning be a musician. Yet, they object to Sara for wanting a nose that is not typically black. Why deny their inalienable right to inconsistency? How could any of us live without it?

She seems very relaxed but says, "I'm really excited today, doc. Do your thing." Sara has her intravenous line running into the back of her hand.

We take her into the operating room and get her set on the table. After I scrub and come into the room and go through the usual procedure of putting on gown and gloves, I prep her nose—I wash it off with antiseptic solution. I do this also for her entire face.

After I drape her, I inject the local anesthetic, but only after she has received Valium and morphine intravenously. She becomes drowsy, and, like many patients, she repeats herself, telling me a few times that her boyfriend is downstairs to take her home.

Many patients fear intravenous medicine, believing that they will reveal some terrible secret. In more than two decades of using this kind of anesthesia, I have yet to hear anything remarkable.

I make a small incision on the columella, the vertical part of the nose that goes from its tip to the lip. With blunt dissection, I make a passage from the base of the columella over the entire top of the nose. This tunnel will receive an L-shaped piece of plastic, silicone. Although I usually prefer material from the patient's own body, I could not get enough cartilage from inside the septum to build up the nose, and I would have to take more from elsewhere, perhaps the ear.

Another possibility would be to use bone, from the hip, but the disadvantages are a visible scar on another part of her body and the possibility that the bone graft will later resorb, disappear.

The silicone I plan to employ is easier, but it is not without danger. Because it is a foreign body, there is the risk of infection, but if that should happen, I could easily remove the implant. One cause of infection is the use of too much silicone, to try to achieve a "perfect" result, thereby causing excessive pressure on the skin. One has to be satisfied with an outcome of A or A− instead of A+.

The strut I plan for Sara is soft but strong enough to raise the tip and increase the dorsum of the nose. Before inserting it, I make incisions inside the nose laterally and introduce chisels to fracture the nasal bones and to bring them inward.

Patients often tell me in the office before operation that they want "enough anesthesia so I can't hear the hammer when you break my nose." The fact is that, even though a patient may hear the mallet striking the chisel, he or she is so obtunded and tranquilized that the sound arouses no anxiety, and sometimes it is even forgotten. Sara does not seem to mind the sound and never mentioned it as a worry.

With the nasal bones now narrower, I insert the silicone without any difficulty and close the incision with fine nylon stitches.

To reduce the nostrils' flare, I remove a small piece of skin and cartilage from the floor of each nostril. As I bring the sides of the defect together with stitches, the nostrils become less wide and less flat.

The new profile of the nose is what Sara wanted. The tip is higher, and so is the bridge of the nose; thus far the silicone has done its job. Nevertheless, a good operation does not necessarily mean a good result. Complications such as infection and shifting of the implant can happen. With Sara's implant, infection is more likely to occur around the seventh to the fourteenth postoperative day. Antibiotics are of questionable value, and I have not used them.

I apply a dressing of tape, but not too tightly, because I do not want to cause pressure on the skin that could lead to an ulceration and loss of the silicone.

Now that her ordeal is over, Sara visibly relaxes. Still looking calm after the operation, she says, "I can't wait to see what you did."

"You'll have to wait until next week. Call the office for an appointment for next Monday, and I will see you there."

I make out a prescription for codeine (she is allergic to Demerol). Sara will be able to go home in an hour or two.

I think more about her motivations for the operation. I do not believe she has undertaken this procedure to flee her blackness. Not every Jew, for example, who has a rhinoplasty is trying to hide his or her religious affiliation. As a matter of fact, having the shape of one's nose changed is a popular operation in Israel, where anti-Semitism is not likely to be a concern. Although every culture has its concept of facial beauty, the Anglo-Saxon ideal has diffused throughout most of the world. I am told, for example, that Eurasian models are in great demand in Asia.

In these instances, plastic surgery is available to better the appearance of those already with good looks. But, to others who may have a deformity or a detested feature, plastic surgery represents freedom. It can break the manacles of ugliness.

A society allows this to happen by having people like me and others with similar skills available. Note, I did not say "freely" available, since an individual may have to insist on an operation to improve appearance and may have to pay something for that procedure. Our society has not yet solved the problem of how much beauty or even normalcy it should grant or give its members. Cosmetic surgery for a big nose is the financial responsibility of the patient. But, if someone were born with a gross deformity, the kind helped by craniofacial surgery, insurance would be more readily available.

Like Sara's family, some people consider a plastic surgical operation an affront; to others, it is an indulgence. We are more apt to draw a closer line around somebody else's entitlement than around our own. We are quicker to seek gratification or relief for ourselves than to grant it to others.

chapter 10

It is now time to change into street clothes. I feel my motor slowing. To revive myself, I resort to hydrotherapy, a shower. I also shave, remembering that what impressed me as an adolescent during World War II was that General Douglas MacArthur, even on Corregidor, allegedly shaved daily to avoid looking harried and unkempt—to assure his troops that he thought all was going well. While I do not have a MacArthur complex, I believe that patients, particularly those awaiting a cosmetic operation the next day, would prefer that the surgeon not look like a survivor. Patients, not surprisingly, are very concerned about their doctor's health. Many want to be sure I am not tired and request that they be first on my operating schedule. Although it is not an unreasonable request, not everyone can be first. In most hospitals, we surgeons are beggars as far as getting on the schedule.

Patients also have another fear: that their surgeons may

drink excessively or stay up too late. Once a patient called me at home to find out whether I was there and when I planned to go to bed. One might have predicted that she was in the hospital for a facelift.

Since I do not like alcohol in any form, no patient need worry about me in that regard. I do recall an embarrassing incident, however, when I advised a woman in her sixties, from whose face I had just excised a basal cell cancer, to take Tylenol with a "cocktail" for pain.

"Doctor, I am a Seventh Day Adventist," she said reproachfully, undoubtedly thinking that I was a hopeless sot.

Although it is now slightly past seven o'clock, later than when I usually finish, I do not go home immediately. I want to see Louise Brewster. Mat, the chief resident, and Andy Johnson, an intern, go with me. That the operation is not the end of the patient's care is an important lesson for any surgeon to learn and remember.

Louise looks surprisingly comfortable. Her parents are with her. She knows the intern and resident, but I introduce them to her mother and father, whom they have not met. This amenity has become a casualty of modern hospital life. Too often the patient must witness a parade of nameless medical personnel who enter the room, stare, ask a few questions, and abruptly make a U-turn out.

Louise says that she has only a little pain but considerable nausea. Nausea following operation is not unusual. It is so common that the medical profession has accepted it too readily, almost as a necessary sequela of general anesthesia. Hopefully, someone will discover a way of sparing patients this unpleasant experience, which, when it occurs, usually lasts six to twelve hours.

In four or five days, after I remove the drains from Louise's wounds, she will be going home, barring a complication.

How one discharges a patient is very important. I prefer to do it myself and do not consider it simply a bureaucratic exercise to be left to the residents and the nurses. The patient also prefers to see me at the time of discharge. It gives us both a sense of closure. After all, I saw Louise when she first came to my office, then when she entered the hospital; I did her operation, and I shall see her at least once every day, and more, if required. I will be there when she is ready to leave, in order to give her instructions about her dressings and about what she can and cannot do and when.

After we leave Louise's room, the residents want my opinion about one of their patients. Supervising residents is an important part of my work and my life. Mat, who is nearing the end of his two years of plastic residency training and has had four previous years of general surgical residency, has his own patients, and they consider him their doctor. We, the attending staff plastic surgeons, are there to be as active in the management of the patient as necessary. He discusses with us every patient on his service and every operation that he does. His judgment is excellent; he knows when he needs help and when he doesn't. He feels no need to prove himself; he is confident, not cocky. In this regard residents differ, as do philosophies of training. Some residents prefer to make the great surgical leap, doing more than they should without proper supervision. This kind of sink-or-swim training occurred more in the past than now, when malpractice suits have become so frequent.

Nevertheless, today the resident must still be able to operate on his or her own. Recognizing the proper time in relation to a specific procedure is part of the responsibility of every head of a surgical service. Anyone who has gone through a residency will remember precisely the occasion when the chief let him or her do the operation without the chief even being in the room. That event is the equivalent of a bar mitzvah.

Mat and Andy now take me to see Billy Patten, a forty-year-old paraplegic whose tragedy began with a gunshot three years ago. His plastic surgical problem is a large pressure ulcer over his hip. Mr. Patten was completely well until he made the mistake of picking up bread at the corner store, then in the process of being robbed. A bullet fired by one of the holdup men struck him in the spine, and that was the end of Billy Patten as he then knew himself. He is black, and his life, which had never been easy, is one of despair. Little wonder that he blots out reality by occasionally drinking himself senseless and forgetting to turn himself every couple of hours to avoid skin breakdown. Hence the ulcer he now has.

The residents know Billy better than I, since they have taken care of him during his frequent admissions to the hospital for the same problem. I am now in Billy Patten's room. I look at him and think of Emerson's phrase, "a fragment of a man," despite the fact that Billy is smoking a cigar and does not seem despondent.

He greets me. "Hello, doc, I am back again." He says this as a statement of fact, without a scintilla of sadness.

"I realize that, Billy. What can we do to help you remember to stay off your rear end so you won't develop these ulcers again?"

"I try, doc. I try," he says without conviction.

We have turned Billy over and removed his dressing. The ulcer is massive and eventually will require rotation of skin and muscle to close this defect. What he will need first is persistent wound care, daily dressings, and debridement, the removal of dead tissue.

Billy seems to be enjoying the hospital. He likes the attention of the nurses and doctors. What some patients consider to be annoying interruptions of their rest and sleep, he views as social visits. Billy even likes the food, a certain sign of how dismal things must be for him at home.

Before Billy leaves the hospital, he will get to know several roommates. The present one is an elderly Jewish bookseller for whom the written word is supreme in his life, religion, and work. Billy reads nothing except the daily menu. He does not bother even with a newspaper. He gets to the outside world through his television set.

The residents and the social worker tell me Billy lives alone but has a friend, Nellie. He makes it clear that she is just a friend. She is married; at least she wears a wedding ring on the appropriate finger. I have seen her a few times when she has visited him. She always brings him cigars, one of the few enjoyments left him.

Bad luck has made Billy a crippled spectator of life. It goes on and goes by him. He has adapted to his enforced passivity better than I think I could. I realize, however, that making predictions about what people can or cannot do under stress and in catastrophe is notably inaccurate.

People are generally stronger than outsiders or they themselves think. Admittedly, some paraplegics engage in such self-destructive behavior as drinking and driving or not turning over and then getting skin ulcers. But rarely does a paraplegic commit suicide by more direct means, such as a gun.

Billy has found something to look forward to. He told a resident that, although he does not get much disability money, he has enough to pay for a woman's personal services once a month. Money well spent, as far as I am concerned. I am not sure that a female social worker from the welfare department would be so enthusiastic as I about underwriting this activity. But that woman, God bless her whoever she is, is Billy's soul food.

For the World War II RAF pilots whose faces he had reconstructed, Sir Archibald McIndoe, the great English plastic surgeon, arranged a party one night and hired prostitutes for the occasion. McIndoe's superiors severely reprimanded him, but he had recognized that the ultimate test of reintegration for those about to return home would be whether someone, paid or not, would couple with them. Even though the women whom McIndoe provided were earning their wages, their willingness to be physically intimate with those men whose faces had been devastated was crucial to the men's rehabilitation and the rebuilding of their self-esteem. A feminist might say that, for those men, the woman existed only as a sexual entity. Perhaps. Yet, if man and woman did not regard each other that way at least on occasion, our species would no longer exist.

When the residents and I leave Billy Patten's room, we discuss his problem. I concur with their plan to operate next week and to rotate a flap of skin and muscle to cover his large open area.

I then call my wife to let her know that, finally, I am on

my way home. Almost always, I return to my sanctum in time to have dinner with the family. Today I am unusually late. My wife, judging from the sound of her voice, is disappointed, but she is not angry. She has always supported me in putting the patient's needs before hers or even mine, but I try not to make my family, and ultimately myself, pay the inordinate price of my professionalism.

This hour of the day frees me from professional unselfishness. I now think directly of my needs and those of my family. For the first time in twelve hours, I feel I am living for myself. No posturing. No guilt. But at the same time, my self-indulgence has its limits. I do have a family, and they have needs. For me to discard my armor and expect to receive and not to give would be a foolish act of self-entitlement. However, it is hard not to become an expectant dependent after 5:00 P.M.

My wife, Roberta, and I are of the past generation. We both considered my being a surgeon a privilege more than a burden. We got married when I was a junior resident at the Peter Bent Brigham Hospital. I was in my second year of training, and she had graduated from Radcliffe. She then went on to get her master's degree in social work at Simmons, while I spent three more years at the Brigham, finishing my general surgical residency.

She also encouraged me when I decided to become a plastic surgeon. This step required an additional two years of training, which, as I mentioned, was in Pittsburgh. My wife continued as a medical social worker in a hospital there until our first child, Linda, was born at the beginning of my final year of residency. After we returned to Boston, I went on with my career, but she interrupted hers. The several years she was at home were not easy for her since she missed being active professionally.

Four years after Linda was born, Laura followed. When Linda was nine and Laura five, my wife returned to the labor force as a psychiatric social worker at McLean Hospital, an affiliate of Harvard Medical School. She enjoys what she does and spends additional hours at home completing reports and telephoning patients' families.

Our children have had the example of parents who work hard. While this may have been good for them, they did not have a mother and father with nothing to do but share unfilled hours with them in play.

As I am about to leave Billy Patten's floor, I see a herd of worried nurses and residents rushing into a room on the neurosurgical ward, where a middle-aged man with an unresectable, incurable brain tumor has had a fatal cardiac arrest. For someone with his illness, this is probably the best way to exit.

Yet his death disquiets me. He is my age, and I wonder about his wife and children, imagining their reaction to the dreadful phone call. I remember too clearly as a resident having to shatter someone's life with the worst news that most of us could receive.

As we become older, we expect death more. Our ranks thin, and we learn to insulate ourselves from the deaths of others.

We have friends who give summer evening parties in their backyard. When I first arrive, the fluorescent light that attracts and electrocutes insects disturbs me. Perhaps my reaction is instinctive or, in my particular case, is the result of having spent time with Albert Schweitzer, who revered all forms of life. Soon, however, despite his tutelage, the zap becomes an inconsequential constant in the background, like the indistinct mutterings of those at a nearby table. Yet how would I react, I wonder, if it were possible to amplify the sounds of an insect's final agony? If these little creatures had vocal chords, I like to think that we would not so easily forget them. Yet I realize my hypothesis is not likely true since I can ho-hum away the deaths of those patients not under my care. The personal link is a crucial determinant of our reaction to the death of someone else. Witness our lack of concern about most people in the obituary section of the paper. If we never knew them personally, we do not think much about their passing, unless he or she was famous.

What is hard for us to comprehend and accept is that at our deaths, others will behave as we do now.

Most plastic surgeons, unless they do a considerable amount of head and neck surgery, do not daily come into close contact with the dying patient. Furthermore, it is unusual in plastic surgery to cause the death of a patient, since they are generally well at the time of an elective procedure.

But I recall Don Foley, whom I killed indirectly. I had treated him when he amputated the end of his index finger at work. He required a flap of tissue from the chest to rebuild the missing fingertip, and twelve days later the flap, being able to survive on the blood supply from the finger, was divided. His sensation at the tip was abnormal, but he still had enough for the army recruiters. A year later, his mother telephoned to say that he had died in Vietnam. She said, "You and he got along so well, and whenever he wrote, he always mentioned you." So, I thought, after I put down the phone, if he had never come to me or any other reconstructive surgeon, he might have been alive today. I tried to console myself by thinking that most of medicine is intervention to postpone the inevitable, which may come either at the expected time or sooner, rarely later.

I am more preoccupied with death than is my wife. My children are fortunate that at least one parent does not have mortality on the mind. Yet, believing that I would die early, like Byron and Keats, has made each hour and day of my life keener.

Although the presence of dying and death is what one sees, and what I should expect, in a hospital, I sense it more this evening because on my way out I see Ann Marie Williams, who is a nurse. Many years ago, her father came to me because of recurrent sweat gland cancer of his nose. He had had three previous operations, but the tumor continued to grow and invade. Removing it would require taking away his entire nose and most of his cheek, without much prospect of cure. Nevertheless, because it was his only chance, Mr. Williams accepted it after the oncologists had concluded that further irradiation and chemotherapy would be useless. He was then sixty-five years old, a policeman about to retire. He had seven children, all of whom either had finished or were starting college. His wife worked as a bookkeeper. Their family life was strong.

With each operation, Anne Marie's father felt he was being eaten away by his tumor and by his surgeons. When he looked in the mirror, his ugliness overwhelmed him. "No one would ever want to have to look at me," he once said. Over the next two years, his tumor required our taking his eye, his orbital bone, and a large portion of his right cheek and sinus. He and we knew we were fighting an impossible enemy. His allegiance to the church, however, was firm, and his faith held. If he wondered "Why me?" he never asked his priest or his doctors. Though a gregarious man who liked to go out for a beer and to see the Red Sox, he clung to home.

"I am no longer what I was," and he was right. His family circled this strickened member. It was no surprise, almost a relief, when he died. That his last moments were at home was also predictable. His wife sent me a letter after his death.

Joe died like he lived, with all of us around him. Even though what he went through was horrible for him and for all of us, I guess the Lord gave us the opportunity to show our love for each other. That does not happen often for most families and we are grateful for that.

When I think of Mr. Williams, I remember less the man whose remaining eye stared from the surgical wasteland and more the person who was able to take life's worst after having had some of its best. That Ann Marie went into nursing to care for the terminally ill is what I would have expected.

As I write about her father, I personify his cancer. By giving it human qualities, albeit bad ones, we make it familiar to us, possibly controllable—anything for hope. The cancer is "the enemy"; "it attacks"; it "eats away"; it is "relentless and insidious." Depending upon the doctor's political stance, the cancer is either a Communist or a Fascist. But the fact is that all disease is neutral; it is an "it." It does not reason, feel, plot, or take pleasure; sacrifice will not appease it. One cannot offer the cancer of one person in the hope of sparing another. But there is always the possibility that even the worst cancer might weaken its stronghold on the victim. I would not argue with a hospital chaplain about why a patient has had a remission. But when the battle tilts the other way and the patient worsens, the ordeal of maintaining faith intensifies for the patient, the family, the physician, and even perhaps for the clergy.

A physician to a dying patient must assess and reassess how much truth that person can tolerate. The doctor's hope is that the patient will accept death for what it is; yet the same patient, when well, seldom thought that he or she was actually dying every twenty-four hours that slipped by. Though we are all condemned, we seldom think of it in that fashion, because we do not know our execution date.

Not only the patient has difficulty reconciling to death; frequently the physician has even more trouble. Perhaps, for some of us, the choice of a medical career, which involves understanding the biological processes of life, was a subconscious reaction against our dread of death.

Death, for most of us, is the ultimate reality, and reality is a concept or entity that most human beings, whether physicians or patients, have difficulty in accommodating.

Although I try to select patients for elective surgery who have realistic expectations, I recognize myself as a dream dispenser. Despite my disclaimers, many patients harbor secret hopes for transformation. My observation is that most people want more than they can get or you can give them. We talk about the ideal patient, someone who has a visual, intellectual, and—most important—emotional understanding of the physical changes that he or she is likely to obtain through an operation, as well as how this change will actually affect the rest of his or her life. But the dream goes on. Most women who have had their faces lifted or their eyes done and now look less tired, perhaps younger, will still want to look that way long after the procedure, even though the surgeon has told them—and they have told themselves—that their improvement will be short-lived.

From forty to seventy years of age, millions fight the external signs of a normal, basic life process. By seventy-five or eighty, if they have lived that long, most of them have given up; they have accepted aging in terms of appearance but not necessarily in terms of death. If they truly believed in a hereafter, maybe they would be more philosophical about dying. In Valhalla, however, they have no guarantee that they would look younger or better. Justice may be as elusive in the next world as it is in this. One might again occupy the ugly end of the spectrum.

chapter 11

It is dusk. My auto stands alone and forlorn. Most of the doctors have gone home. Although I am late to leave, I enjoy the pleasurable release that comes from having worked hard and thinking that I did my best. All went as well as I could reasonably expect. I have no lingering sense of error or tragedy. Satisfaction is what I feel, not elation.

Weariness for me is no stranger. It is a gentle leveler, flattening my emotional peaks, inducing calmness, fostering relaxed self-appraisal. Now is one of the rare times of the working week when I can take a long look.

A few days ago, a patient seeking correction of her small, sagging breasts asked me what operations I like to do, a question she probably took from a magazine article with a title like "How to Choose Your Plastic Surgeon."

I told her I like doing whatever procedure I schedule and that frankly I have the luxury of refusing patients if I do not believe either they or I are right for the operation. I also said that it would be a rare plastic surgeon who would admit to a prospective patient that he or she disliked an operation that person wanted.

My patient persevered, looking no longer at her list of questions, but at the wall and my certificates. "You are certainly successful, and you must enjoy it."

I admitted to being busy. I dislike hearing the word "successful" applied to me, since I immediately associate that adjective with the commercial aspects of my work. Yet, in truth, I would not enjoy being described as "unsuccessful." If I had been completely honest with that patient, I would have admitted that I like whatever "success" I have had, until I get harried and tired. My achievements then become an engulfment. I feel cornered, fixed on the golden spike, skeletonized like the great fish in Hemingway's tale. I dwell more on the pressures of medicine than its privileges. Routine murders romance. Like most guards at art museums, I become oblivious to the opportunities for personal growth that my surroundings offer. In my instance, I am apt to neglect the uniqueness of each of my patients. On Monday of a usual week, I begin like a physician, but by Friday I sometimes consider myself a short-order cook.

Aside from the demands of my career, the fact that I am an active observer-participant in my own life can be wearying. Introspection seldom is exhilarating. There is much to scrutinize and assess in what I do, because there are many choices. Unlike the completely programmed giant atlas moth, which has no mouth or digestive system and devotes the ten days of its adult life solely to mating, I am an organism of sufficient complexity to have other things to do and consider beyond procreation. Like most human beings, I also realize the implication of today becoming tomorrow: time lost, chances missed, tasks undone, expectations unmet—all in a step toward death. Yet every day is important to me, although no day is ever finished. As Leo Stein said about Cezanne's paintings, "There can scarcely be such a thing as a completed Cezanne. Each canvas is a battlefield of victory, an unattainable level."

Curious how often we use military terms to describe civilians who are relentless in their work and determined in their goals. In medicine, for example, we frequently say, "He fights for his patients" or "He marshaled his consultants." And I did describe myself, half-seriously, half-comically, as a knight—but of the operating table (which isn't round). At this time of the day, my emblem would be a wilted rose.

A warrior, even if he is victorious, can perish on his return from the fray if he is careless. I have in mind more than falling off one's horse or colliding with another car. I am talking about being ambushed. For medicine today, that analogy finds expression in the malpractice suit.

At times like this, driving home, I think more of the risks of what I do than when I am in the process of taking care of my patients.

In 1984, the estimate was that every physician in the United States during his or her professional lifetime will become embroiled in a malpractice claim. I became that statistic some time ago. That the case crept along for seven years before going to trial is testimony to the labyrinthian inefficiency of our legal system.

I do not want to present all the details of my ordeal, but

the plaintiff, an elderly woman, alleged that I had been negligent in my treatment of a lesion of her nose and claimed that I had subjected her to excessive surgery. What reverberates most intensely in my mind from the two and a half days in court is not so much the verdict, which was in my favor, but the unpleasantness of the experience. I am sure that the plaintiff did not relish it either.

Even though I knew that thousands of physicians each week must contend with malpractice suits, I could not react phlegmatically to the accusation of "negligence." It was a startling affront to me, as I pride myself on acting always in the best interest of the patient. Admittedly, I am not free of error, but negligence—never! Or so I thought.

To prove malpractice in Massachusetts, the patient must prove negligence. The plaintiff must show that the doctor did not behave according to the customary and accepted standards of care by physicians of a particular category, in my instance, plastic surgeons.

The law also states that the result of treatment is not necessarily a proof of negligence. A bad scar, for example, does not necessarily mean that it arose from negligence. In addition, since many physicians differ in their treatment, an alternative course of action taken by a physician is not per se a negligent one.

As my trial approached, I had Kafkaesque thoughts: I should confess to a crime I did not commit, in order to end the ambiguity that I detested.

The night before going to court, I relied on my usual defense (and I do not mean my attorney) against anxiety and tragedy: humor. I realize that this commodity is not the exclusive property of Jews, but we have evolved a special brand for our large, unwanted experience with adversity.

At bedtime, I asked my wife where she had put my "striped pajamas." What I was doing, of course, was imagining the worst possible outcome of my trial, a jail sentence (an impossible consequence), so that any judgment against me, which my insurance company would have paid, would seem inconsequential.

My recounting my trial is similar to another's describing his operation. Being in court for me was like being in the hospital for a patient: neither of us would willingly choose the experience if we could get the result by other means. Those who come for a cosmetic improvement consider the surgery a last resort, and the operating room an undesirable place to spend an afternoon.

During my trial, which I wildly imagined to be a modern auto-da-fé, I jotted down a few words that characterized this experience.

NAKED: I felt stripped and vulnerable, as do my patients when they must submit to examination and operation. When the attorneys privately delved and publicly delivered facts about me and my work, it reminded me of how we physicians, even if caring and sensitive, can embarrass patients by presenting personal information about them on our rounds.

SHAME: I was mortified about having to defend myself in an open forum against charges that depicted me as a bad physician. I felt sullied, as do my patients who are ill. Although being sick can happen to anybody, many are ashamed of what they consider a defect or a taint: cancer, tuberculosis, psychosis, venereal disease. Despite my intellectual acceptance of the fact that any physician can be sued, I still reacted with shame.

As I was walking to the courthouse one morning, I saw

a neighbor approach. Instinctively, I jumped behind a tree until he had passed. I did not want to tell him what I was doing there. I then thought of my patients who try to hide their recent cosmetic operations. When some ask what they can tell their friends, I glibly advise that the best tack is to be truthful. "After all, a lot of people have this type of procedure," I usually add, almost automatically.

The fact that trials are commonplace in our society and that other doctors go through them every day really did not make a substantial difference in my reaction to my situation.

IMPOTENCE: The large courthouse, the enormity of the legal process, its impersonality, and my unfamiliarity with it made me feel powerless, as do most of my patients who go into a hospital, an operating room, or even my office. My survival in court, like my patients' survival in surgery, depended largely upon the skill of others. For me, my fate belonged to my attorney, the plantiff, the plaintiff's attorney, a few witnesses, the judge, and most importantly, the jurors. I felt that I had little control over any of them. I surrendered myself to another person's care, my attorney, and hoped that he would be a true professional, which he was.

Many times during the trial I recalled telling patients, "Don't fight the system; relax with it; we have been there before, and we know how to take care of you and your problem."

In fact, my attorney said the same thing to me.

I was determined to be a good client, in the same way that many patients say that they will be "good."

When my attorney complimented me on my "courtroom behavior," I felt proud, like a child.

Adding to my sense of powerlessness was the realization that luck is a hefty factor in the outcome of any trial. Are the jurors intelligent? Do any have a grudge against doctors? Is the judge fair and knowledgeable? Will my attorney be up for this one?

I thought of the remarks that many patients make before operation:

"Doctor, will the anesthetist be experienced?"

"Make sure you get a good night's sleep. Don't fight with your wife and take it out on me [nervous laugh]."

"I want you to do the cutting and sewing, doctor. I realize it's a teaching hospital, but I came to you because I know your reputation and I have confidence in you."

"Doctor, I am really scared, because anything could happen."

DISCOMFORT: Although my trial did not inflict physical pain, it certainly was no Caribbean cruise. I experienced emotional discomfort and somatic malaise. My attorney told me that he would try to make the court sessions as "least unpleasant" as possible for me, just as I frequently tell my patients, "Although you will have pain with the procedure, I will give you something to lessen it and hopefully it will not be a bad experience for you."

The most tormenting part of the trial for me was listening to the plaintiff's attorney systematically building a case against me in his summation to the jury. While I understood that he was acting on his client's behalf—and doing his duty—I felt anger toward him, probably unfairly. Yet I also realized that he was there not to help me but her.

To show how primitive my thinking had become, I resented him, a Jew, taking up the cudgel against me, also a Jew—all that for a contingency fee!

Witnessing what I considered his distortion of the truth pained me even though I realized that attorneys must present their best arguments to the judge and the jury. However, hearing him attack my judgment and skills and my not being able to respond was hard to endure. I could not stop the pain, just as a patient on the operating room table under local anesthesia occasionally must bear the discomfort until the ordeal is over.

Physiologically, with pain that is continuous, one develops a merciful numbness. I felt less pain with each day in court and with each minute that the opposing attorney spoke.

I was aware that the court, like a hospital or an operating room, is a paradigm of routine that in itself provides a peculiar kind of relief. For the uninitiated, there is the security of realizing that thousands, even millions, have gone through this before and somehow have emerged.

I soon fell into my role as a defendant, just as others did as plaintiff, attorney, witness, judge, juror.

A distancing occurred. I became an observer of myself as a participant. I could at will take myself outside the verbal fray, away from the courtroom. Patients have described to me a similar sensation when they have had to go through extreme pain.

The mind transcends the body and both rise above the noxious event. I existed between a dream and a nightmare. I was floating, and below I saw the enormous courthouse and, within it, the courtroom—now small—with all of us, tiny figures, involved in an ancient rite. I then had the thought that the courthouse existed less to promote justice than to combat injustice, just as a hospital has more to do with disease than with health.

Although the trial lasted just two and a half days, it was so enervating that thoughts of vengeance gave way to feelings of fatigue. In my reduced, spacey state, the verdict seemed to lose much of its importance.

Yes, I confess, I did have fantasies of what I would do or not do should the plaintiff or her attorney suddenly need a doctor. Nevertheless, I never doubted that I would act like the physician I think I am.

Unbelievable, I thought, that a simple operation on the nose of one person still in excellent health could have unleashed such an extraordinary chain, involving so many people, so much time, so much paper. There is something either very wrong or very right with our society that it can expend so much for so little. And to do it so seriously while paying insufficient attention to real injustice, to those who are black, hungry, disenfranchised. How many starving people could the costs of my court trial save? How many scholarships could it provide? Irrelevant, I realized, but not completely so, if one has more than a mole's view of human suffering.

But I could not fault the lawyers and the courts for having taken themselves seriously even in minor matters. That is exactly what doctors and hospitals do for patients, and that is what patients expect.

The jurors, though not professionals, behaved like professionals, with seriousness and respect for their duties. I never saw them before and probably never will again, but they entered my life at a critical time.

On the last day of the trial, I did not wait for the verdict. If it were against me, I would not have wanted to be there to receive it. And if it were unfavorable to my patient, I also did not want to view her degradation. Seeing someone demeaned has never given me pleasure.

For a while after the happy verdict, I felt elated, but then let down with the realization that it was not a victory, merely a reaffirmation that I was not negligent, something I believed anyway.

So I had won a test that left me what I was, and if I had lost, I would not have ostensibly surrendered either face or finances. But something worse might have happened. I might have thought differently of my patients. I might have become, at least for a while, more wary of them and more withholding. I hope that I would have had enough insight to recognize that I would be penalizing the majority because of a single incident. I would also be injuring myself by increasing my cynicism about human beings. As a species, we are peculiar: we make war, but we seek peace; we maim each other, but build hospitals to care for our victims. I must agree with the Chinese proverb: "There is all animal in man but not all man in animal."

To a young surgeon who wishes to enter my specialty, do I mention my trial? No, unless our conversation veers toward it. I would not wish to discourage him (or her) from becoming a plastic surgeon. He might miss a life that would be good for him and good for others, one that frequently would make him tired but never bored, that might give him several unpleasant hours but many more fulfilling years.

Even though some days have more irritants than pearls, I am fortunate to be doing work that calls forth the best in me and demands still more, that takes enough time so I do not need to initiate ersatz projects to justify my existence, that directs my selfishness to include others, that pays well, earns respect, that might permit me to make a small difference in this world.

I admit from time to time that I do console myself over

the fact that no museum will ever have a retrospective of my work for posterity to remember. My human canvases will have desiccated into nothingness along with me. Balzac was right: surgeons are only "heroes of the moment."

I am sure that most of the jurors at my trial envied me, despite my temporary predicament, for what they imagined must be the quality of my life. They probably would have been surprised to learn that many plastic surgeons protest against "the pressures" we have.

True, but look at the stresses on most people. They must work hard, and most will remain economically precarious. Perhaps those who have been exploited, dispossessed, and wronged will be recompensed before they die, or soon afterward. But while they are waiting and wobbling on this earth, I will try to do whatever I can for them.

Through fate and choice, my position is a plastic surgeon on a bridge that joins me to my simian progenitors. While trying to comprehend the paradox of being at the same time something and nothing, I take comfort in knowing that whatever I have done or will do with my life and my time has provided a continuity, fragile and unspectacular to be sure. Yet there can be no tomorrow without me and my generation today.

I often feel the exquisite sadness of my transitory role. Eventually someone else will occupy my place and in turn will surrender to another, probably not graciously, not without a fight to prolong for a mini-instant his or her time on this planet. As for me, I may die with the names of loved ones on my lips, or perhaps, like a worn-out Dr. Chips, I will see certain patients pass in review—Louise Brewster, Rose Dember, Ida Gelkin, Billy Patten.... But while I am here in palpable form, I still shall seek the road to Louveciennes, as Sisley painted it in summer. And, if I am fortunate, someone else will be with me helping me across the moats.